MODERN ARNIS

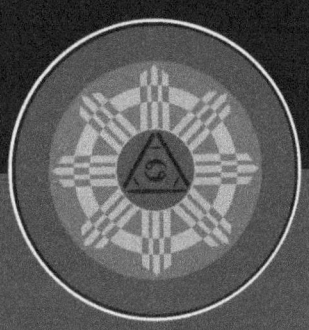

HISTORY & PRACTICE

Mag Aaral

MODERN ARNIS: HISTORY & PRACTICE
Copyright © 2018 by Mag Aaral
—First Edition—
ISBN-10: 0-9980654-0-4
ISBN-13: 978-0998065403

All rights reserved. No part of this book may be reproduced in any form without prior, written permission from the publisher or author, except in the case of brief quotations in articles or reviews.

The material in this book is intended for educational purposes only. No one should undertake the practice of self-defense or healing without qualified instruction and supervision, and an awareness of the criminal and civil limitations on the use of force in self-defense and the practice of medicine. Physical combat is an inherently dangerous activity. Medical diagnosis and treatment should be provided by qualified healthcare professionals. The author, publisher, and distributors are not responsible in any manner for any injury or liability that may result from practicing—or attempting to practice—the techniques described herein. Any application of the information contained in this work is at the reader's sole and exclusive risk. Because of the danger of injury to oneself and others, prior to engaging in any type of self-defense program it is advisable to consult both a professional martial arts instructor and a licensed physician.

This book was printed in the United States of America by Stirling Bridge Publications; a publisher specializing in works dedicated to exploring the power of one.

stirlingbridge@mail.com

For Professor Remy Presas—

World-class fighter,
Master instructor,
Founder of Modern Arnis.

Your guiding hand is sorely missed...

TABLE OF CONTENTS

	Foreword	1
I	Introduction	3
II	Origins of the Art	7
III	The Professor	12
IV	Presas Family Style	20
V	Balintawak	28
VI	Shotokan Karate	31
VII	Kodokan Judo	34
VIII	The Council	37
IX	State of the Art	43
X	The Final Days	46
XI	Choose Your Weapon	48
XII	Choose Your Target	55
XIII	Choose Your Method	62
XIV	Use Your Body	73
XV	Double Cane	78
XVI	Empty Hand	85
XVII	The Forms	88
XVIII	The Flow	92
IXX	Friends, Family, and Followers	94
XX	The Future of the Art	166
XXI	The Words of the Grandmaster	168

FOREWORD
Dr. Remy Presas Junior

This book is about my father and his art of Modern Arnis. The editors have asked for, and received, my family's blessing to write it.

The goal of this book is to reach out to everyone who has made a contribution to the art. Its purpose is not to demean anybody and not to try to tell anybody who to follow.

Papa was a humble man. He told us to 'walk with our feet on the floor,' and not to try to elevate ourselves above anybody else. You could see this in the way he would work with everybody, regardless of how advanced they were.

He also taught us that if you can't say something nice, don't say anything at all—just keep your mouth shut and let your stick do the talking!

I support the goal of this book. In my view, if anyone has made a contribution to the art of Modern Arnis, that's good for me, because it is my family's name. And in the end, as my father used to say, "It is all the same!"

—Dr. Remy Presas Junior, July 17, 2014

MODERN ARNIS PRINCIPLE: LET THE STICK DO THE TALKING.

Dr. Remy P. Presas, Jr., is the head of MARPPIO—the Modern Arnis Remy P. Presas International Organization—based in the Philippines.

I. INTRODUCTION
Maligayang Pagdating!

Remy Presas was taken from us too soon. While he is now gone, the lessons he taught remain, shared out among several generations of Modern Arnis practitioners (arnisadors) all over the world.

⊗ For those who did not have the opportunity to know him, this work is intended as an introduction to the man and his art.

⊗ For those who did know him, it presents familiar material, but perhaps from a slightly different perspective. Among the Professor's students are members of several different organizations, in various states and countries, each of which is dedicated to practicing and preserving his art. It is unlikely that these disparate branches of the common root will ever be united under the same banner again, but here, in this book, representatives of most of them have come together in the spirit of cooperation to share memories of their teacher and insights into the art he taught.

⊗ And for those who knew and loved him, this book may be a walk down memory lane and a chance to compare notes with others whom the Professor welcomed into his extended family.

The first part of this book explores the origins of Modern Arnis, beginning with the Presas family style, progressing to the influence of the Balintawak School, Shotokan Karate, and Kodokan Judo, and culminating in the cross-pollination of this art with those of other Grandmasters after the Professor came to the United States.

The second half of this work presents some of the core skills of the Modern Arnis curriculum. While it is in no way intended as a substitute for the direct, personal instruction through which this system is properly taught, it may serve to whet the appetite of those who are new to the art, and perhaps give more advanced practitioners a few tidbits to chew on.

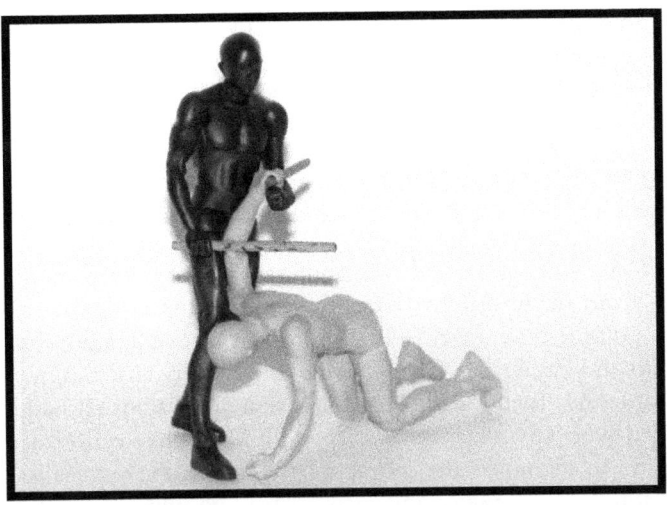

†—	Attacker (sword symbol) [*lusob*]
⊕—	Defender (shield symbol) [*depensa*]

ARNIS, KALI, OR ESCRIMA?

What is the difference between Arnis, Kali, Escrima (or indeed Eskrima), Estoque, Baston, and so on? In many ways, the answer is, 'not much.' While there are, of course, differences from system to system, these various terms can essentially be used interchangeably to reference the indigenous cane and empty hand fighting arts of the Philippines. Or as the Professor would say, *"It is all the same."*

He chose to use the term "Arnis" because it is a word that both comes from, and is widely recognized throughout, the Philippines. In this way, it pays appropriate respect to the culture from which it sprang. And while he did not know it at the time he christened his art, it would also be the primary term employed in the 2009 law officially making Arnis the national martial art of the Philippines.

ARNIS

One final matter should be addressed by way of introduction: when asked about his inspiration in creating the art of Modern Arnis, Professor Presas often said that it was based in large part on his realization that the student and the teacher are more important than any given style or name.

> **MODERN ARNIS PRINCIPLE: THE MASTER-STUDENT RELATIONSHIP IS PARAMOUNT.**

This book is comprised of contributions from many of the Professor's students, from many different countries, and many different styles. Each provides a different perspective on the student-teacher relationship that was so dear to the Professor. With that in mind, individual ranks, titles, and systems are rarely mentioned. These deliberate omissions should in no way be equated with any absence of respect. Rather, they reflect a conscious effort to try to minimize any distractions based on the appellation, lineage, or affiliation of the *messenger*, and focus instead on importance of the *message* itself…

FILIPINO WARRIOR

II. ORIGINS OF THE ART
The Universal Flow

So where did it all begin? So much ink—and indeed blood—has been spilled over the ages in pursuit of the answer to this seemingly innocuous question, in a wide variety of contexts.

The Philippines: The earliest written 'document' from the Philippines is the Laguna Copperplate Inscription, created in the year 900 A.D. In addition to evidencing the existence of a thriving culture in that region while Europe was still in the grip of the Dark Ages, it also reveals cultural linkages between the Filipino people and various Asian civilizations, notably, the Javanese Medang Kingdom, the Srivijaya Empire, and the Middle Kingdoms of India.

THE LAGUNA COPPERPLATE INSCRIPTION

✗ Notable to arnisadors is the Inscription's use of the term: *'dayang.'*

ARNIS

Undoubtedly, the Filipino tribal warriors of this era had already developed their own, indigenous fighting systems, but it would be a narrow-minded world view indeed that ignored the effects of cultural cross-pollination commonly observed in the evolution of the fighting systems of virtually every nation in history.

Java and Sumatra: Pencak Silat was practiced as early as the sixth century by the inhabitants of the Srivijaya Empire on Sumatra and by the eighth century by citizens the Medang Kingdom in East Java. Silat is a full-body fighting system that employs striking, grappling, throwing, and weapons. It was practiced by the Indonesians not only for self-defense purposes, but also for the psychological and spiritual benefits it conferred.

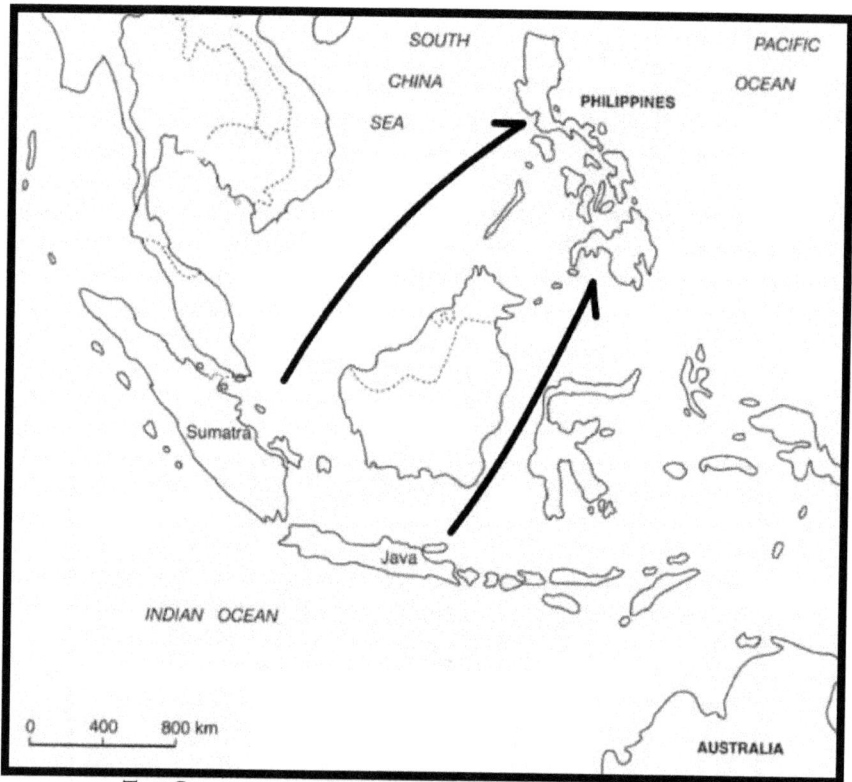

THE GEOGRAPHY OF FILIPINO MARTIAL CROSS-POLLINATION

India: Kalaripayattu (a combat system that employs striking, kicking, grappling, forms, weapons, and healing methods) and Silambam (a primarily stick/staff based fighting art), in turn, had been evolving for almost a thousand years by the time the Indonesians first began practicing Silat.

SILAMBAM PRACTITIONERS

The legend of the monk, Bodhidharma, who introduced these Indian martial practices to the priests at China's Shaolin Temple is well established. A less-well-known corollary espoused by several eminent martial historians, however, posits that the fighting methods of Bodhidharma's homeland had their own origins, in turn, in the Greek art of Pankration, introduced to India by the army of Alexander the Great during its three hundred year occupation of the subcontinent beginning in the fourth century B.C.

And so the martial tide flowed from shore to shore, and coursed down through the years and centuries…

MODERN ARNIS PRINCIPLE: IT IS ALL THE SAME.

Spain: By the time the Spanish conquistadors landed on the shores of the Philippines in the sixteenth century, the local inhabitants were well-versed in blade-based martial arts. It was with just such a weapon—and an art—that Datu (chieftain) Lapu-Lapu killed Ferdinand Magellan at the Battle of Mactan in 1521, forcing the much more technologically advanced invaders to retreat and regroup.

Opinions vary widely regarding the degree to which Spanish fighting methods influenced the post-invasion development of Arnis. It is undeniable that much of the Filipino art's nomenclature—including its very name[x]—has Spanish origins, but this may be more the result of the fact that Spanish was the *lingua franca* of the Philippines until the early twentieth century, than any technical influence Spanish fencing techniques actually had on the art itself.

> **THE VOYAGE OF MAGELLAN, JOURNAL OF ANTONIO PIGAFETTA (1525)**
>
> *...An Indian hurled a bamboo spear into the captain's [Magellan's] face, but the latter immediately killed him with his lance, which he left in the Indian's body. Then, trying to lay hand on sword, he could draw it out but halfway, because he had been wounded in the arm with a bamboo spear. When the natives saw that, they all hurled themselves upon him. One of them [Lapu-Lapu] wounded him on the left leg with a large cutlass, which resembles a scimitar, only being larger. That caused the captain to fall face downward...*

LAPU-LAPU AND MAGELLAN AT THE BATTLE OF MACTAN ISLAND

[x] Arnis comes from 'arnés'—Old Spanish for armor. Likewise, 'harness' is an archaic English term for armor, which comes from the same root as the Spanish term.

From this historical perspective, then, a few things are clear:

⊗ Like virtually every other fighting art, Arnis is the descendant of a variety of martial ancestors.

⊗ It has several cousins, including Escrima and Kali.

⊗ And it has sired a number of lines of its own, among them, the Modern Arnis of Remy Amador Presas.

Since the loss of Professor Presas in 2001, many members of the Modern Arnis branch of this ancient tradition have gone their separate ways. But out of respect for the Professor, his style, and the art in general, it is important to remember that what unites us is *so much more* than what divides us...

THE MACTAN SHRINE (DATU LAPU-LAPU)

ARNIS

III. THE PROFESSOR
There Is One Way—My Way!

Remy Amador Presas was born to Jose Presas and Lucia Amador in the tiny fishing village of Hinigaran in Negros Occidental, Philippines, on December 19, 1936.

HINIGARAN

In Tagalog, the family name is pronounced: "Preh-sas," not "Pree-sas" ("Preh-" as in "red," not "Pree-" as in "green").

Young Remy was introduced to Arnis early in life by various relatives, starting with his grandfather, Leon. This was to be the beginning of his lifelong love of the martial arts, and he proved to be a gifted and dedicated student. In his early teens, he left home to study different fighting systems and test his mettle in competition, both within and outside the ring.

At that time and place, street fights (*bakbakan*) were a common occurrence, and whenever Remy was challenged in this fashion, he regularly prevailed. In addition, he frequently entered stick-fighting tournaments that were typically held at local *fiestas*. These were full contact competitions in which the combatants did not wear armor or use padded weaponry. Because of his superior abilities, Remy always walked away with the prize money!

In 1957, at the age of twenty-one, Remy began teaching Arnis out of a small gymnasium in Bacolod City, Negros Occidental. It was here that the innovations the world would one day come to know as Modern Arnis first began to take shape. It was also during this time that he met his first wife, Rosemary Pascual, whose assistance and insights were to have a profound impact on the development of the art.

REMY AND ROSEMARY

ARNIS

> Because Remy was functionally ambidextrous when wielding the cane, many who trained with him did not realize that he was actually left handed—at least not until it was too late!

Beginning in 1961, the young stick-fighter studied and taught at institutes of higher learning. First at La Salle College (in Negros Occidental) and then at the University of Negros Occidental, Recoletos, he instructed classes in Shotokan Karate, Kodokan Judo, and Greco-Roman Wrestling, while at the same time pursuing his own academic studies.

UNIVERSITY OF NEGROS OCCIDENTAL (UNO) RECOLETOS

Students during these early years recall that Remy would often integrate stick-fighting techniques into his classes, even though Arnis was not, strictly speaking, part of the syllabus.

By the end of this chapter in his life, he had earned a bachelor's degree in Physical Education and senior rank in the Japanese martial arts (sixth degree in Shotokan Karate and *dan* ranking in Kodokan Judo that was to culminate at fifth degree). Interestingly, it was in the academic, rather than the martial, context that Remy first came to be called, "the Professor."

In 1969, the Presas family moved to Manila, the island nation's capital, where they rented a three-story building, the second floor of which served as a martial arts school: The National Amateur Karate Organization.

MANILA

Why not the National Amateur **Arnis** Organization? The answer to this question lies at the very heart of the evolution of Modern Arnis: Because at that time the Filipino arts were not nearly as popular as Chinese and Japanese fighting systems, in large part because stick-related injuries were so common. One of the primary things that made Modern Arnis *modern* was the revolutionary idea that practitioners should strike stick-on-stick rather than stick-on-hand, as had previously been the custom. This seemingly simple innovation dramatically improved student recruitment and retention in an art that many characterized as 'dying' prior to the Professor's emergence on the scene. And it was this modernized version of Arnis that the Professor began layering into his classes in the Japanese martial arts.

MODERN ARNIS PRINCIPLE: MAKE THE INNOVATION.

Studying and teaching both Japanese and Filipino systems of self-defense over the years inspired the Professor in a variety of other ways as well. For example, his creation of Modern Arnis as a discrete martial was accompanied by the adoption of a formal ranking system, specific titles, and an official uniform.

The first rank structure of Modern Arnis was as follows:
Likas (green belt)—*Likha* (brown belt)—*Lakan* (black belt)

ARNIS

THE ARNIS UNIFORM

In the early years of the following decade, Modern Arnis was on the rise:

⊗ In 1970, the Professor created the International Modern Arnis Federation (IMAF).

⊗ In that same year he gave the first of what would be several demonstrations of his art to audiences in Japan (including the police).

FILMING IN JAPAN

⊗ In 1974 he authored the first book on Modern Arnis (and one of the first books about Arnis of any kind).

⊗ In this same year, he served as the martial arts consultant on the Dean Stockwell movie: *The Pacific Connection.*

⊗ This was also the year he immigrated to the United States in order to escape the very real danger of continuing to teach Arnis without submitting to the newly-mandated authority of the military government in such matters.

REMY AND JOSE PRESAS AT THE AIRPORT

ARNIS

After coming to America, the Professor continued to teach his beloved art on the seminar circuit; sometimes alone, sometimes in the company of other luminaries of the martial arts world. For many years he lived the nomadic life of an itinerant master, having no permanent address and eschewing the trappings of an anchored life. At times, the longest he stayed in any one place was during the week-long camps that were to become an educational staple for his first generation students in North America.

NEW ENGLAND SUMMER CAMP, 1996

Intensive Modern Arnis Camps were regularly held at various venues across the United States throughout the 1990s. These martial conclaves typically lasted from several days to a week or even two. Training began right after breakfast and continued throughout the day, often lasting late into the night. Learning—both on and off the mat—occurred at a dramatically accelerated pace in this environment of total immersion, and bonds were forged that remain strong to this day. Videotaping was frowned upon, if not, banned outright: technique was expected to be absorbed organically; not frozen in a glass box. Those who were fortunate enough to attend will always remember how special these gatherings were.

⊗ In 1982, the Professor was named Instructor of Year by *Black Belt* magazine.

⊗ In 1994, he was selected by this same publication as the weapons instructor of the year.

REPRODUCED WITH PERMISSION FROM *BLACK BELT MAGAZINE*

In 2000, the Professor was diagnosed with brain cancer. In February, 2001, he 'escaped' from hospital to attend a training camp in Philadelphia. It was to be his last. On August 28 of that same year, Remy Amador Presas crossed over to the farther shore and joined the pantheon of the past masters. He was survived by his first and second wives, Rosemary Presas and Yvette Wong; his seven children, Mary Jane, Mary Ann, Remy (Junior), Maria, Demetrio, Remia and Joseph; and an extended family of friends and students all around the world.

ARNIS

IV. PRESAS FAMILY STYLE
Could You Do That?

Remy Presas' grandfather—Leon—fought in the Spanish-American War of 1898. His father—Jose—served as a Lieutenant in the U.S. Army during Second World War. Accordingly, in addition to having a venerable martial heritage, his was also a family with a proud military tradition.

DEMETRIO, MARY ANN, ROSEMARY, JOSE, REMY, REMY JR., MARY JANE, AND MARIA

Three days after Remy's fifth birthday, Japanese troops invaded the Philippines. Like many others, the Presas family took to the mountains outside Negros Occidental to hide from the attacking army. In these extreme circumstances, young Remy was captivated by the sight of his father teaching the ancient fighting methods of his people to fellow soldiers in the flickering light of the guerilla campfires.

Because of his tender years, the family tried at first to dissuade Remy from taking on the study of such a dangerous and deadly art. But when it was clear that he would not be deterred, his grandfather Leon—a veteran of another war and an experienced arnisador—took on the training of the young warrior. And so it was at this time and place that the man who was to become one of the world's leading authorities on the Filipino art of stick-fighting took up the cane.

MOUNT KANLA ON NEGROS OCCIDENTAL

Among the first techniques Remy learned from his grandfather was *abanico* (the fan movement). In time, he would expand upon the existing *largo* and *corto* variations to create his own innovation: *abanico doble action*. This, and many other methods that Remy first learned at his grandfather's hand, have passed directly into the curriculum of Modern Arnis.

ARNIS

When the Second World War ended, Remy was nine. He returned to school for a time, where he was frequently disciplined for fighting. One day a staff member realized that it might be better to channel the young warrior's energies into positive pursuits, so he was made a kind of school prefect. Truancy, theft, and other such problems were resolved overnight!

Every day after school, Remy practiced his art while kneeling under the low ceiling in the basement of his family's home.

⊗ At the age of twelve, he witnessed a bloody duel between two brothers who were students of a famous wartime guerilla.

⊗ At thirteen, he and his cousin Jorge stowed away aboard a boat bound for the island of Cebu—a martial arts mecca—where some relatives on the Amador side of the family lived, in search of adventure. There, he met a powerful stick fighter from the Balintawak tradition: Rodolfo Moncal. This encounter was to have a profound effect on the young fighter.

THE PORT OF CEBU

In Cebu, Remy studied the Balintawak system (discussed in greater detail in the following chapter) for several years under a variety of instructors, including the legendary Venancio "Anciong" Bacon.

⊗ By the age of fourteen Remy had already begun developing into a very strong fighter, knocking out a sinawali master with a single blow.

ARNIS MASTERS IN CEBU

⊗ In his late teens, Remy parted ways with Bacon and the Balintawak system and returned to Negros Occidental (for reasons discussed in the following chapter).

⊗ In 1957, he opened the first Arnis school in his province. If the mountains of Negros Occidental were the place where Modern Arnis was first conceived in the mind of a young Filipino boy, this was its birthplace.

THE BROTHERS PRESAS

Remy may have become the most well-known arnisador in the Presas family, but he was not the only one. His two younger brothers, Ernesto and Roberto, both became masters of the cane as well.

ERNESTO PRESAS

ARNIS

Ernesto Amador Presas was born in May of 1945. His father, Jose Bonco Presas, a renowned Arnis fighter in the area, began teaching Ernesto the fundamentals of Arnis at age eight. A capable learner, he mastered his lessons well and soon expanded his martial arts education to include the study of Judo, Jujitsu, Karate, and eventually Kendo.

In the time-tested custom of Arnis practitioners of that era, Ernesto trained intensely and fought many challenge matches against other practitioners. One memorable encounter in 1970 saw him facing an Arnis fighter from the Manila suburb of Paranaque, who wanted to test the skills of the upstart who had just moved to the city from a rural area. The two fought in a rice paddy, where lateral movement was severely limited, and falling into thigh-deep mud was a distinct possibility. They began with a trial to see who could disarm the other of his stick. Using his complete knowledge of levers and disarming methods, Ernesto successfully took the other fighter's stick away in two successive clashes. Not satisfied with this turn of events, the other fighter insisted on an all-out skirmish. Ernesto went on to disarm his foe once again and delivered a rain of blows that knocked his opponent into the mud.

Other fights would follow, with the frequent condition that the other fighter was always the challenger—Ernesto did not seek conflict, but never backed down from it either. Because his knowledge was not limited only to combat with weapons, Ernesto also bested karate practitioners while fighting barehanded, including one opponent who fell into the river the two were struggling near after Ernesto pounded him with hard punches and kicks. These battles, he would later divulge, formed an important facet in the development of his comprehensive fighting system.

In 1972, Ernesto secured teaching positions as a physical education instructor at the University of Santo Tomas, the University of the Philippines, Far Eastern University, the Lyceum of the Philippines, and Central Colleges of the Philippines. He also began teaching Arnis at military and law enforcement institutions including the Philippine National Police Academy, the Far Eastern Military Academy, the General Headquarters Military Police Academy, and the Officers' Schools for the Philippine Army and Air Force.

During those formative days, the Arjuken Karate Association held classes from Monday through Saturday and also held special events and demonstrations on Sundays. Arnis classes featured basic training in groups, with students executing blocking, striking, and disarming techniques with single or double sticks. Sparring was practiced both with and without the use of protective equipment such as headgear, body armor, and gloves. Equipment allowed students to make hard contact, while sparring unprotected called for more controlled action as only rattan sticks were available (the soft, foam sticks later developed in the U.S. for training and tournaments would never gain popularity in the Philippines). Instruction on anyo (forms) and practice with bladed weapons were largely conducted on a one-on-one basis because of space limitations and for safety reasons.

In addition to the Arnis classes, students could learn JKA-line Shotokan Karate, Ju-jitsu throwing and locking skills, Okinawan weaponry (tonfa, bo, nunchaku and sai), as well as Kendo. (There exists today, particularly in Australia and Canada, a system known as Arjuken karate, popularized by early Ernesto Presas students). Ernesto was a firm advocate of cross-training, as he believed that this better prepared the student to deal with the greatest variety of possible attacks and weapons. Exponents of other martial arts could often be seen visiting, observing, and practicing alongside the school's regular students. Ernesto Presas passed away in 2010.

ROBERTO PRESAS

Roberto Amador Presas was born in 1947. He holds a lakan sampu (10th degree) ranking in Arnis and has taught martial arts to the Philippine Air force, AFP/PNP, U.P. Police and Marikina Police among others. On occasion he is contracted to teach the national martial art of Arnis to students in public and private schools of the areas in and around Hinigaran. Grandmaster Roberto Presas heads the Philippine Arnis Hinigaran Association. Recently he was approached by the mayor of Hinigaran to demonstrate his art at public events sponsored by the City of Hinigaran.

After the loss of both parents Grandmaster Roberto began training with his brother Remy. He said his brother Ernesto wasn't interested in training in the beginning but eventually joined in and all three trained together. His brother Remy later took on a job relocating him to Cebu where he trained with a few different groups and later establishing his own path. This left Grandmaster Roberto training and working with his brother Ernesto. He spent years living with and training with his brother Ernesto, he taught classes for him in his school. Later Grandmaster Roberto left Manila and returned to Hinigaran.

Since the death of his brother Remy in 2001 Grandmaster Roberto Presas is the recognized highest ranking man in the IMAFP, followed by Grandmaster Cristino Vasquez, and then Grandmaster Rene Tongson. He is no stranger to the challenges of life. Born with a cleft palate and slight hearing loss, Grandmaster Presas has had to work harder at communicating but seems to get his point across just fine. He has weathered the years. He has a rugged appearance and a gleam in his eye. Put a stick in his hand and he bursts into life. Don't let his size fool you, at about 5' tall he commands the floor with high energy. His footwork is quick and penetrating. He prefers the straight line Japanese style over the Okinawan half circle

Grandmaster Roberto's favorite weapons of choice are the *baston* (cane) and the *nunchaku*. He was amazing to watch when in his younger days. He has slowed down a bit now with age and some health issues but still gets out and moves with authority on the workout floor. Grandmaster Roberto is the true embodiment of the family system, a genuine and absolutely the real deal. The Grandmaster has a representative in the United States who is helping build Hinigaran Arnis De Mano by teaching and spreading the Art. He is Guro Kurtis Goodwin of the A.P.I. International Combat Arts Association in Portland, Oregon. Grandmaster Presas's wish is: "to spread my art to everyone interested... I am happy to share my family style."

—**Steven K. Dowd** and **Kurtis Goodwin**
Reprinted, with thanks, from the FMA Informative

Over the years that followed, Remy taught his family art, complemented by what he had learned in the training halls and on the streets of Cebu, at various academic and martial institutions throughout the Philippines. In 1974 he immigrating to the United States and, from that time forward, he traveled the county, and indeed the world, spreading the art of Modern Arnis.

After the Professor's passing on August 28, 2001, many individuals and groups continued to teach Modern Arnis, or variations thereof, all around the world. Within the Presas family, Remy's brothers—Ernesto (until his own death in 2010) and Roberto continued practicing and teaching their own styles of Arnis, and the Professor's son—Dr. Remy Presas Junior—is now the head of MARPPIO: the Modern Arnis Remy P. Presas International Organization.

Outside the Presas bloodline (which term is used as opposed to "family" because the Professor often told his loyal students, "you are all part of my family now"), many other groups practicing Modern Arnis under the direction of Masters of Tapi-Tapi, Datus (chieftans), and high-level black belts, can be found in the Philippines, the United States, Canada, Germany, and many other nations.

While these various factions do not always see eye-to-eye on particular issues, they are united by their love of the art, and it is the hope of the Editors, the aim of this work, and the expressed desire of the Presas family that all who walk in the Professor's footsteps can come together here, in these pages, in the spirit of comradeship, if only for a brief moment, to pay respect to the founder of their common, martial lineage.

MODERN ARNIS PRINCIPLE: THOSE WHO TRAIN IN MODERN ARNIS ARE FAMILY.

V. BALINTAWAK
The School of Hard Knocks

When Remy first arrived in the city of Cebu in 1949, there were two main stick-fighting schools in existence: Doce Pares and the Balintawak Street Self-Defense Club.

- Doce Pares ("the Twelve Pairs") was a confederation of cane-masters from many different styles, named to honor its twelve founding members and to echo the Twelve Paladins of the Emperor Charlemagne.

- The Balintawak Club, by contrast, was named for the street it was on.

The common denominator of these two systems was the legendary Venancio "Anciong" Bacon. Originally one of the most skilled members of the Doce Pares Club, Bacon broke from this well-established organization over disagreements regarding its combat effectiveness, and founded the Balintawak Club. Balintawak is a realistic, no-nonsense, close-quarters art, in which practitioners box with both empty hands and sticks.

BALINTAWAK CLUB: VENANCIO BACON SECOND FROM RIGHT

> **Rodel Dagooc** sometimes says that in order to perform certain techniques properly, you need to be "close enough to kiss your opponent!"

At the time when Remy first studied it, some of those sticks were tipped with metal, and, as a result, many practitioners could be recognized by their missing teeth! There was no ranking system beyond student-teacher, and lessons were primarily conducted one-on-one.

It is fair to say that the Balintawak School attracted some of the most dangerous individuals in the region. Violent and sometimes deadly street fights designed to test the mettle of the school and its students were not uncommon, and Bacon was one of the toughest ever to pick up a cane. This made him an attractive target. On one occasion, Bacon actually killed an assailant by snapping his spine; an act which resulted in a judicial acknowledgement of Bacon's martial expertise and a lengthy term of incarceration.[✕]

> **MODERN ARNIS PRINCIPLE: UNDERSTAND HOW TO APPLY TECHNIQUE 'IN REAL'.**

✕ Undeterred by this involuntary change of state, Bacon continued to train and teach his art in prison. Upon being paroled, he returned to the Balintawak School, where he taught for the remainder of his life.

ARNIS

For a young arnisador seeking his fortune in the big city, the choice was easy: Remy was a Balintawak man. He trained in this system for many years, first with Rodolfo Moncal and police major Timoteo Marranga, and eventually with Venancio Bacon himself. Remy learned early on that when he visited Bacon for training in the evenings, plying him with *Ginebra San Miguel*—a favorite alcoholic drink in the Philippines—helped to facilitate the flow of information...

Like all good things, Remy's close association with Venancio Bacon eventually came to an end, but he left Cebu to go his own way with the master's blessing. It is fair to say that the teachings of the Balintiwak School had a profound effect on the young fighter—and also that he made quite an impression on its members during his time there. Elements of this hard-hitting tradition comprise a large part of the foundation on which Modern Arnis was built, as can be seen, for example, in the Professor's 1-2-5-12 drill.

THE BALINTAWAK STREET SELF-DEFENSE CLUB, VENANCIO BACON CENTER

To this chapter one more thing must be added: There is an idea in some circles within the Filipino martial arts community that one can be *either* a strong fighter *or* a good teacher. Remy Presas was both. The tough street-fighter who prevailed in countless full-contact matches on the mean streets of Cebu was at the same time a kind, patient, and highly effective instructor. In this—as in many other things—the Professor defied limitation.

VI. SHOTOKAN KARATE
You Will Learn The Way

One of the most amazing aspects of the Professor's method was the way he could integrate his art seamlessly into any other system. He called it, "finding the art within your art." This ability may have had something to do with the fact that he learned—and taught—Filipino fighting methods alongside various other systems, most significantly, Shotokan Karate.

> **MODERN ARNIS PRINCIPLE: FIND THE ART WITHIN YOUR ART.**

Shotokan (the house of the pine waves) Karate was developed by Gichin Funakoshi in the first half of the Twentieth century. Like most traditional styles of Japanese martial arts, it is comprised of *kihon* (basics), *kumite* (sparring), and *kata* (forms). At advanced levels, *bunkai* (interpretations from kata) are taught, which include *tuite jutsu* (joint manipulation) and *kyusho jutsu* (pressure point striking). The Twenty Precepts of Shotokan stress respect, compassion, and patience. Shotokan employs a belt ranking system which was initially comprised of only three levels.

ARNIS

GICHIN FUNAKOSHI

The first rank structure of Shotokan Karate was as follows:
8th-4th *kyu* (white belt)—3rd-1st *kyu* (brown belt)—1st *dan* (black belt)

All of these characteristics have parallels in the Professor's art. Modern Arnis was a twentieth century take on an ancient martial tradition. Its founder adopted standardized nomenclature and uniforms and promulgated a simple belt-ranking system. While its historical roots are in sparring and free-fighting, students are also taught basic techniques, patterns, and forms. In particular, the form Anyo Apat (Pamalo) follows the same "I-formation" footwork as karate's Heian or Pinan forms.

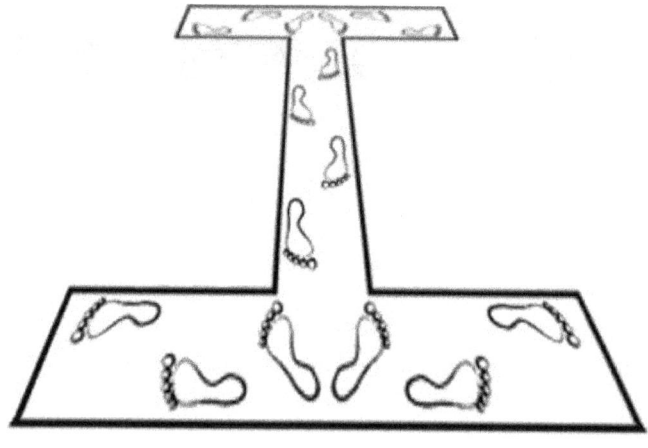

Finally, as anyone who trained with the Professor can attest, he was the most respectful, compassionate, and patient of teachers; a true gentleman. In these several ways, the effect of Shotokan Karate is very much alive and thriving in the syllabus and practices of Modern Arnis.

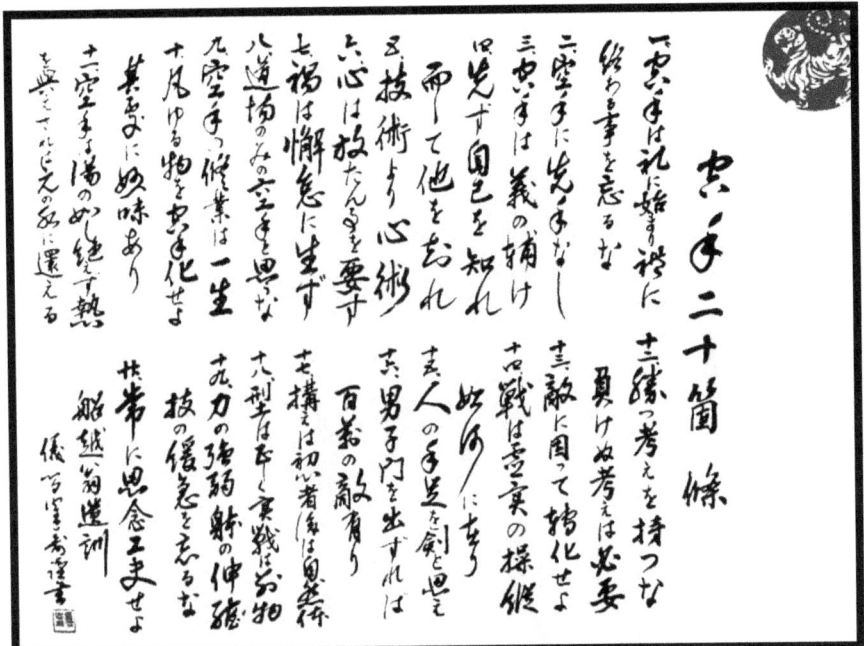

THE TWENTY PRECEPTS OF SHOTOKAN KARATE

VII. KODOKAN JUDO
Ju Yoku Go O Seisu

In addition to earning senior rank in Shotokan Karate, Professor Presas was also dan-ranked in Kodokan Judo. This Japanese art was a natural extension of his earlier experience in Filipino *dumog* (grappling), which he learned from a variety of masters in Butuan, in the Southern Islands, where this sub-discipline is among the first taught to students. Anyone who trained with the Professor can still hear him gleefully announcing "mobility throw!" as he twirled his hapless partner to the ground.

Kodokan Judo was created in the late nineteenth century by Japanese master Jigoro Kano. As a threshold matter, it was Kano who first adopted the ranking system and uniform that was to be adopted half a century later by Gichin Funakoshi for Shotokan Karate, which, in turn, likely inspired Remy Presas to do the same for Modern Arnis three decades after that.

In addition to its trademark throws (*nage-waza*), Kano's art emphasized grappling (*katame-waza*), locks (*kansetsu-waza*), and chokes (*shime-waza*), all of which feature prominently in Modern Arnis.

JIGORO KANO

> As I recall, the Professor was teaching in Japan at the Kodokan and was challenged by a Shotokan Fifth Dan who claimed that the Professor would not be able to throw him. Well, he did. Defeating an opponent of a given rank was one of the ways that promotions were awarded in that time and place, so at the end of the seminar, a group of black belts presented the Professor with his Fifth Dan in Shotokan Karate.
> —Ken Smith

JIGORO KANO PERFORMS UKI-GOSHI ON YAMASHITA YOSHIAKI

In addition, Judo—"the gentle way"—was predicated on both the effectiveness (*seiryoku zen'yo*) and the morality (*jita kyoei*) of avoiding the use of force against force—in other words, the power of "going with the flow," and the importance of avoiding injury to one's training partners. Is this starting to sound at all familiar?

MODERN ARNIS PRINCIPLE: GO WITH THE FLOW.

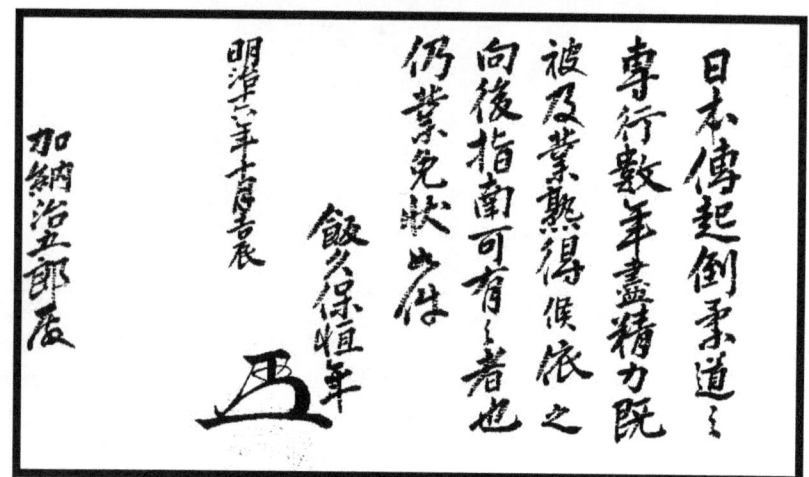

JIGORO KANO'S KITO-RYU JUDO CERTIFICATE

The Professor's studies in Judo foreshadowed events yet to come: Kano's art arose from its more aggressive ancestor, Jujutsu. Both Judo and Jujutsu, in turn, combined to form the foundation of Grandmaster Wally Jay's Small Circle system. Perhaps it was inevitable that the martial tide would bring these two visionaries together one day…

VIII. THE COUNCIL
We Call It 'Sharing'

It was a different time. A time before there was a karate studio on every street corner. A time in which Eastern ways were still largely shrouded in mystery in the West. A time when young people's lives were more real than virtual. During this era, there were only a handful of well-known martial arts masters in the United States, and their scarcity contributed to an atmosphere that was more supportive than it was adversarial.

GRANDMASTERS REMY PRESAS AND LEO FONG TRAINING IN THE PHILIPPINES

ARNIS

In this golden age of discovery, four powerful forces collided, converged, and combined to form a sort of council of elders, which endured for several decades. Now, sadly, half of the founding members are gone. But their story—and their teachings—live on.

It began in 1974, when **Grandmaster Leo Fong**, the founder of the art of ***Wei Kuen Do***, received a call from a movie producer in the Philippines who had read his books and seen him on the cover of *Black Belt* magazine. This producer offered Leo the lead role in two of his upcoming movies, which were to be shot in the Philippines. Eventually Leo accepted and traveled to Manila to begin filming his first movie: *Murder in the Orient* (also released under the title: *Manila Gold*). Leo was treated like a star, and even after filming was completed, he decided to remain in the Philippines for another year. It was during this time that he became a close friend and training partner of Remy Presas.

Their initial encounter took place in a gymnasium in Manila. Details of this historic first meeting vary depending upon whose student is doing the telling, but what is undisputed is that these two masters engaged in a good-natured sparring match where each more than held his own, and from which they both emerged as colleagues and friends. This cooperative, collaborative, and mutually respectful relationship endured until the Professor's passing in 2001, and established the pattern of things to come when Remy moved to the United States the following year and met two more giants of the martial arts world.

GRANDMASTERS WALLY JAY, GEORGE DILLMAN, AND REMY PRESAS

After coming to America, the Professor met **Grandmaster Wally Jay**, the founder of **Small Circle Jujitsu**, and **Grandmaster George Dillman**, the head of his own branch of **Ryukyu Kempo**. Together, these headmasters taught seminars around the country, and indeed the world, for decades, sharing concepts, venues, and students, and learning from each other along the way. The certificates of a very fortunate generation of their students bear the signatures of all four of these martial pioneers.

Although the Professor already had experience with Japan's "gentle way" prior to meeting Wally Jay, the impact of Small Circle principles on Modern Arnis is undeniable. Likewise, George Dillman's Pressure Point theories quickly made their way into the Modern Arnis curriculum. And these colleagues of the Professor rapidly adopted Modern Arnis as part of their own systems' regular practices as well.

> We all felt that we could learn something from each other, and this is exactly what happened. When Remy was teaching sometimes I might jump in, but I didn't know his art. When I would show a guy something, Remy would say, "you know it, you know the arts." It's the principle that's important. We got along really fine. We were never jealous of each other. We taught together in many countries—Europe, Australia, New Zealand, all over the place. Oh, we got along good!
>
> **—Professor Wally Jay**

> A big influence for me was Remy Presas. I ran into him in New York in the 1980s when Dad, George Dillman and he were touring together. I had come on board and begun touring with Dad, and Remy really took me under his wing. He would say, "Wally Jay Junior! Now we go make business!" He would ask me questions and then say, "So what do you think you are going to do next? What is your focus?" I'd tell him, and he'd laugh at me! He say, "You are so naïve!" Remy had the touring thing all figured out and he helped both my father and me in that regard. When we were touring I remember that we'd run into Ed Lake, Chas Terry, Will Higginbotham and all these people, and while Dad, George, and Remy were talking in the front room, we were all in the kitchen until the wee hours working out techniques ourselves. If I could change anything about my martial arts journey I would have spent more time with Remy when he was alive. He wanted me to do more of the Arnis thing with him, but I was heavily into chasing pressure points and couldn't juggle all that, and of course I lived in Europe at the time. Looking back I really could have done more with him.
>
> **—Professor Leon Jay**

ARNIS

In 1974, I was living in the Philippines while working on a movie. That was where I first met Remy Presas. I had joined a local fitness club and I told the man who ran it that I would like to meet some of the local masters. One day he introduced me to Remy. The first thing he said to me was that I should try to kick him! I did, and he trapped my leg and started to sweep me. I figured if I was going down, he was going to come with me, so I grabbed his hair to break my fall, and prepared to do some grappling! He just laughed and said, "Very good—when do we start training?" I said, "tomorrow morning."

Every morning from that day until I returned to California, we trained together. We tried all kinds of techniques to see what would work and what would not. He showed me many things, but at the same time he was humble enough to see if he could learn certain things from me as well. What struck me the most about him was his fluidity—his ability to flow from one move to the next—that is the most important thing I learned from him.

After I returned to the United States, I helped to distribute copies of his book. He always said that he would go to America one day, and that when he did, everyone there would learn about Arnis. He did just that. He was truly a man of vision. He would say if he could imagine something, he could make it happen.

When I later crossed over with him at events and seminars (along with Wally Jay and George Dillman), he hadn't changed—even though he enjoyed his fame, he never lost touch with his humble roots. He was the same old Remy who I had met in the Philippines.

I continued my own FMA training with Angel Cabales of Serrada Escrima, and ultimately combined what I had learned from these two masters to create Modern Escrima[X], which I still practice to this day.

After Remy died, all kinds of people started claiming to be his successor, but, having known him well, I think the best way we can honor him is by humbly practicing his art, living a generous and exemplary life, and seeking our own truth.

—**Grandmaster Leo Fong**

[X] *See* Appendix B: Leo Fong's Modern Escrima.

I attended seminars of Remy Presas, Wally Jay, Leo Fong, and I had them in to my school for seminars. We got talking about technique and we wound up sharing. From the minute I saw Wally Jay on the mat, I knew that I needed his Small Circle for what I was doing. So we started sharing, which led me to Remy Presas and Remy came in, and he started working with me on disarming people—taking weapons away, and I worked with him on pressure points. The three of us had some sessions that I would give anything to have on video. We had some training sessions with the four of us—my wife was in the room—doing and sharing techniques that the average martial artist would find unbelievable. It was fantastic.

Remy—I miss him badly. I always tell people that he was my booking agent. Remy would call me and say: "You and I will teach a seminar. We will do this in Atlanta, Georgia." I'd say, "We will?" and he'd say, "Yes, yes, you must be there!" and then he'd hang up. He did the same thing with Wally and put the three of us together, and it was awesome for almost fifteen years.

—**Grandmaster George Dillman**

PROFESSOR REMY PRESAS AND GRANDMASTER GEORGE DILLMAN

ARNIS

In this way, the ancient voices of the Philippines, Japan, Okinawa, and China united in a four-part harmony, the beauty and power of which far exceeded what any individual, standing alone, could have hoped to produce. And while the circle is now broken, its magic endures...

MODERN ARNIS PRINCIPLE: SHARE WITH EACH OTHER.

IX. STATE OF THE ART
Make It Your Own

Under the Professor's guiding hand, Modern Arnis was an organic art. It is often said that those who studied with him in the 1970s learned a different art from those who were trained in the 1980s (or the 1990s for that matter), particularly when comparing the experiences of students from the Philippines with those in the United States.

> Arnis master, actor, and bodybuilder, the late **Roland Dantes** was a powerful ambassador of unity within the Filipino martial arts community. He was also among the Professor's closest friends.

Even at the brink of the new millennium, one of the Professor's students recalls picking him up at the airport to find him bubbling over with excitement about his latest "innovation," and keen to practice as soon as they reached his hotel room. That was simply the nature of the man and his method.

> ⊗ *TAPI-TAPI/VISIDARIO* ⊗
>
> Unlike many of the other methods within the syllabus of Modern Arnis—the rounded striking form of *redonda*; the sinuous curves of *sinawali*; the lateral sweeps of *banda y banda*—*tapi-tapi* does not follow a specific pattern. Commonly translated as "counter for counter," *tapi-tapi* involves anticipating, and even inviting, a particular counter from the opponent, and then being ready to counter that counter with another technique, often a trap. As a result, it can describe a wide variety of combinations, and even constitutes a general strategy in the realm of the fighting arts. The sequence of initiating (or responding to) an attack, baiting the opponent,

> anticipating his response, and trapping him is sometimes called *'visidario'*—the transformative flow.

Having acknowledged the fundamentally evolutionary nature of Modern Arnis, however, it should be kept in mind that all incarnations of the art are still variations on a common theme, and, as with those who practice these various versions, that there is much more that unites them than divides them. It would be hard to find a student of the Professor's, for example, who did not know the twelve basic strikes, *de cadena* (the trapping hands drill), the various *sinawalis*, the basic forms, and so on—the fundamental tools of the trade, if you will.

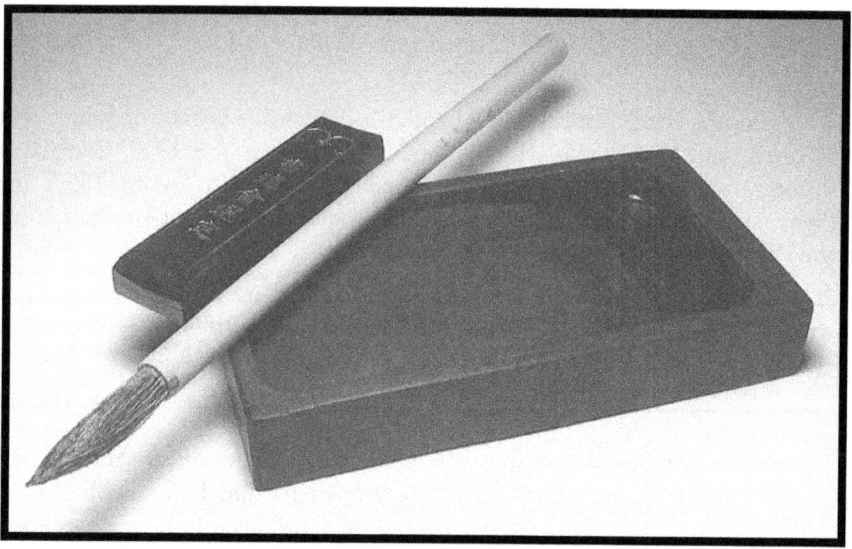

And as any experienced fighter will confirm, it is generally these basic instruments—and not the more complex, advanced techniques—that carry the day in any realistic combat setting.

But the Professor always encouraged his students to "make the art your own," meaning that variations among practitioners were not only tolerated; they were encouraged. Students were expected to use their tools slightly differently from one another; to create their own masterpieces. It is therefore not in keeping with the Professor's well-known attitude toward training to haggle over fine distinctions between one group's approach and another's.

MODERN ARNIS PRINCIPLE: MAKE IT YOUR OWN.

Whenever those who trained with the Professor pick up a stick and swing it with skill, sincerity, and intention, they are treading the path of the Founder of Modern Arnis, and they are also honoring his memory.

The followers of the Professor can be divided up into a few groups:

- There are some who studied with him for long enough that both he and they were comfortable with them breaking off and forming their own art; going their own way.

- There are others who dedicate themselves to preserving the syllabus of Modern Arnis just as it was taught to them by the Professor.

- And there are those whose path lies somewhere in between these two approaches.

Representatives of every major organization which maintains a connection with the art of Modern Arnis were invited to contribute to this work, and all submissions were welcomed. The only requirement was that any material provided had to be in keeping with the Professor's positive, inclusive outlook on the martial arts, and on life in general. The result is a comprehensive overview of the current state of the art.

ARNIS

X. THE FINAL DAYS
I Love You, You Know...

> On the issue of mortality, a wise woman once said there are only three things you need to consider:
> 1. Everybody dies.
> 2. Was it a good life?
> 3. Was it a peaceful departure?

While many thought him indestructible, shortly after the turn of the millennium, the Professor's time came. His life was a wonderful testament to the fact that the martial arts could transport a wide-eyed boy from a tiny fishing village in the Philippines to the world's highest elevations and farthest reaches. And his ultimate departure for the distant shore—while premature—was peaceful.

Unlike a flame that is suddenly snuffed out in the blink of an eye, the Professor had some indication that his time might be growing short; his candle guttered a bit before it was ultimately extinguished. Following his diagnosis, he underwent surgery and spent time in various hospitals. As unpleasant as that period of winding down must have been for a man of such vitality, it allowed him the opportunity to put some of his affairs in order.

In his final months, he 'escaped' from hospital to attend one last seminar in Philadelphia. His arrival caught everyone in attendance by surprise. Amidst the clacking noise and smoky smell of mass stick-on-stick contact, he shuffled, unannounced, into the auditorium. Pair by pair the practice gradually ground to halt. All eyes were now on the Professor and time seemed to slow to a virtual standstill. Tentatively, gingerly, and with the signs of his recent surgery still painfully clear, he made his way from group to group, grasping hands and exchanging greetings with familiar faces. Afterwards he sat on a bench at one side of the room, watching the students practice the art—*his* students, practicing *his* art—like a proud grandfather. For many, it was the most important moment of this, or any other seminar.

Even closer to the end, he placed a series of phone calls to friends and family from his hospital room. One student vividly remembers receiving an unexpected call from the Professor in which they talked about this and that for a few minutes—nothing remarkable—but then the Master ended the call with these words: "*I love you, you know…*"

It was his way of saying goodbye.

MODERN ARNIS PRINCIPLE: YOU HAVE IT ALREADY.

ARNIS

XI. CHOOSE YOUR WEAPON
A Tool For Every Job

Most styles of martial arts teach students to defend themselves with their empty hands before moving on to weapons training at more advanced levels. Modern Arnis follows the opposite path. In this system, students are typically armed from the outset. The theory is that learning how to fight with weapons actually facilitates unarmed combat training. And what a selection there is from which to choose...

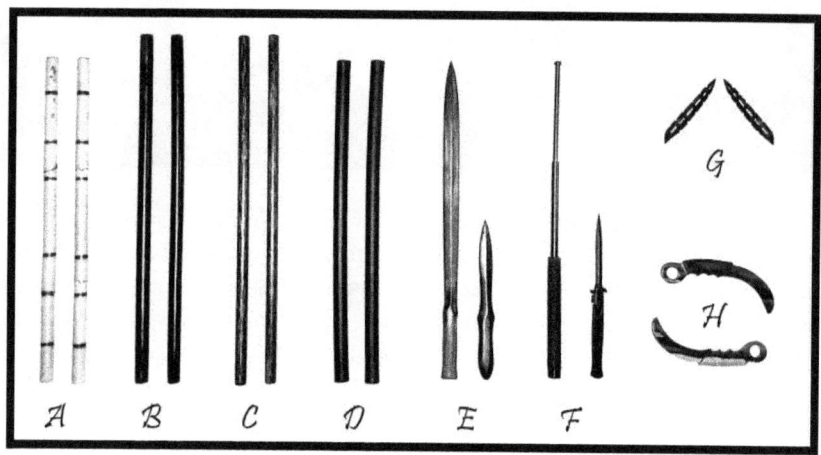

<u>STICK OR BLADE</u>

The first step, then, is to select an appropriate weapon. In most cases, the better practice is to begin with wood. Steel can be very unforgiving. But this is not to suggest that wood cannot be deadly as well. It should be kept in mind that wooden weapons have both saved and claimed many lives through the centuries. Make no mistake: Where steel will cut, wood will crush.

When dueling with steel blades was outlawed in Japan, determined adversaries engaged in "sparring matches" with specially designed bokken known as "gekken," often with lethal results.

⊗ **FIRST LESSON: STEEL CUTS FLESH; WOOD CRUSHES BONE.**

In addition, for those who are learning the art, at least in part, for its practical self-defense applications, the chances of having or finding some item that can serve as a cane—an umbrella, a broom handle, or even a chair leg—are much higher than are those of having easy (not to mention legal) access to an edged weapon. Having said that, however, it is still helpful to remind students from the outset that many of the principles of stick-fighting are based on the blade arts from which it sprang.

For those who wish to focus on the bladed origins of this art from the outset, the wooden knives and swords shown in Figure E provide a compromise solution. Using such training tools helps to avoid the tendency of some newcomers to the art to move the cane in the same way, with the same grip and orientation, regardless of the angle and direction of the particular technique. It helps them to appreciate the importance of cutting rather than merely striking, whether holding an edged weapon or a cane.

Of course, soldiers (including American, Russian, and Indian), law enforcement officers, and other professionals who study FMA to augment actual combat training may need to work up to training with live blades and telescoping batons (like those pictured in Figure F). And senior practitioners of the art will eventually come to know how to use the *dulo-dulo* (Figure G) and the *karambit* (Figure H).^X But for the vast majority of students, a wooden cane is a great tool with which to start.

DIMENSIONS

The Professor was never a stickler when it came to determining a precise length for the cane. This is probably because he was equally effective with sticks of all different shapes and sizes. A good rule of thumb, however, for those embarking on their Modern Arnis journey, is that the weapon should be appropriate to their own body-size.

Some schools suggest measuring from armpit to wrist; others from armpit to fingertip. Either way, the idea is that as an extension of the practitioner's arm, the weapon should replicate his reach. Somewhere between about twenty-six and thirty inches is a typical length for an adult male. Diameters range from about half an inch for children's sticks to an inch-and-a-half for grown-up, heavy-duty contact. A little under an inch is a fairly standard measure.

MATERIAL

In the realm of type of wood, there are several choices:

A. RATTAN

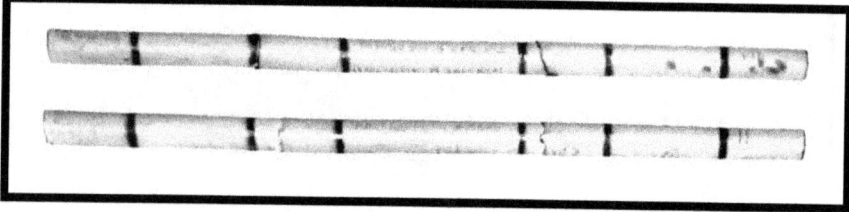

Technically the stem of a vine, rattan is perhaps the best choice for beginners for several reasons. First and foremost, its fibrous composition gives it a built-in safety feature: it will gradually fray with use rather than abruptly snapping, thereby virtually eliminating the danger of flying pieces injuring practitioners. This attribute also makes it a better material with which to defend against an edged-weapon attack.

X As Bram Frank points out, while the *karambit* is often practiced in FMA, it is actually of Indonesian origin. In his own training, he prefers the *bolo* or the *gunting*.

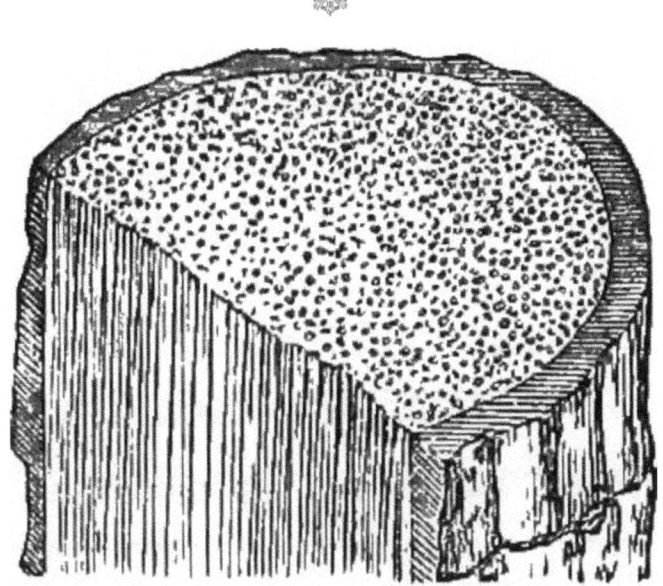

An interesting byproduct of the capillarity of the rattan vine is that air can pass through the length of a cane. As strange as it sounds, blowing hard into one end of the stick will demonstrate this point clearly by extinguishing, or at least affecting, a naked flame at the other end.

ARNIS

Indigenous to the Philippines, rattan is hard and durable, yet lightweight and inexpensive. It is a nodular plant, and many experts contend that the more nodes a stick has, the stronger it will be. Rattan canes are often decorated by burning the tan-colored skin to create darker rings or patterns. Some practitioners even use these decorations to demarcate different 'parts' of the weapon. Rattan is, in many ways, the perfect raw material for making Arnis canes.

B. KAMAGONG

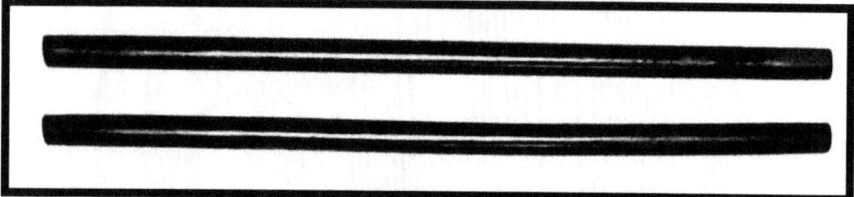

Kamagong (sometimes called Philippine ebony) is a rich, dark, self-lubricating wood that is also native to the Philippines. It is so dense that it will actually sink in water. Kamagong is so hard that it will destroy most other types of training weapons, and even stands up well to metal blades. In fact, it is renowned for damaging woodworking tools while being cut and shaped. Kamagong canes are thus best reserved for solo strength training exercises or use in real combat situations. It should be noted that it is an endangered and expensive species, and is therefore a material that is more appropriate for advanced and dedicated students of the art.

C. BAHI

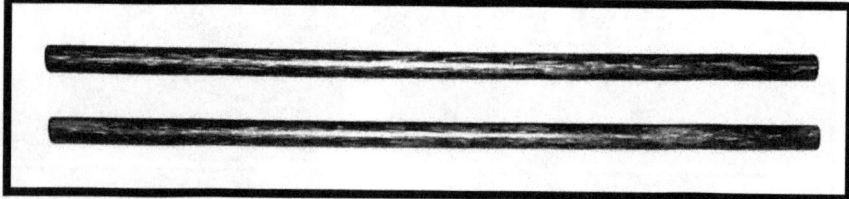

Tiger-striped bahi wood, also known as palm or coco wood, has much of the fraying quality of rattan, but also boasts a good deal of the beauty, weight, and density of kamagong. As a result, many practitioners claim that it provides the perfect combination of speed, strength, and durability. Bahi wood is often the material of choice for duels, which still take place in parts of the Philippines to this day. It too is an endangered species. As a result, the caveats mentioned regarding kamagong apply here as well.

D. Synthetic

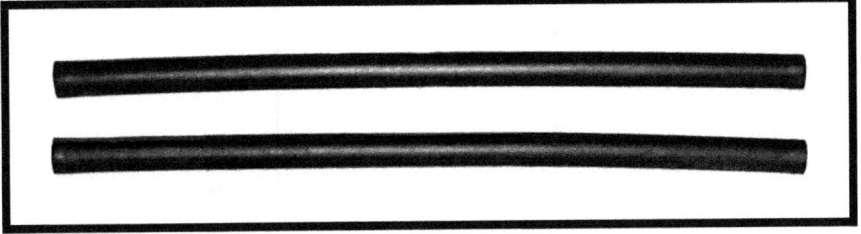

In recent times, a number of more modern materials have been used to make synthetic canes. Leo Fong uses foam padded sticks in his Arnis practice in order to avoid injury when striking vulnerable targets, and also to serve as thin striking shields in empty-hand practice. But while such composites have several advantages over their primal forebears, there is nothing quite like the hypnotic clatter and acrid smell produced by a good, long, session of rattan-on-rattan contact...

SECTIONS

Having selected a cane of the correct dimensions and material, the next question is: what part of the cane should be used to perform a specific technique? It is here that the natural placement of the nodes and the practice of burning rings along the stick at specific intervals can help to landmark some of the different options.

> The cane represented below is presented in the traditional "warrior's orientation" (as opposed to the "noble orientation"); that is, with the handle to the right.

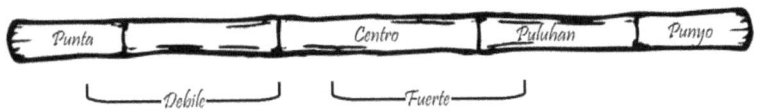

As a threshold matter, it is important to grasp the weapon at the proper grip-point (the *puluhan*), so that a few inches protrude from beneath the hand. This vital extrusion—the *punyo*—can be used to perform a variety of techniques, including traps, locks, and strikes. Care must be taken, however, to ensure that the *punyo* is long enough to be used against the opponent, but not so long as to be used *against* the practitioner *by* the opponent. Most practitioners agree that a little less than a hand-width is ideal.

Arnis

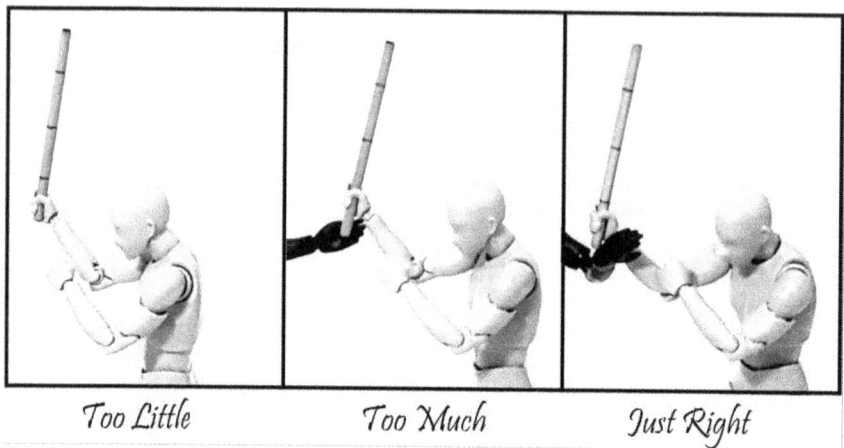

Too Little   Too Much   Just Right

While the tip of the weapon (the *punta*) is used for thrusting, strikes should aim to make contact a little further down the stick (what is known as the *debile* in fencing) so as to avoid missing altogether. Meanwhile, passing moves, like *palis-palis*, should be accomplished using what fencers would call the *fuerte*. And the middle of the cane—the *centro*—can be used very effectively to crush and choke, especially when the practitioner grips both ends of the weapon.

> ⊗ **SECOND LESSON: CHOOSE YOUR WEAPON.**

XII. CHOOSE YOUR TARGET
Know Where To Go

ARNIS MASTERS FROM A BYGONE AGE

Now that the practitioner is armed, is holding the cane correctly, and knows which section to use, the next step is target selection. There are traditionally twelve primary targets in Modern Arnis:

THE TWELVE BASIC STRIKES [PLUS THREE]

1. Forehand strike to *opponent's* left temple (*striker's* right side);

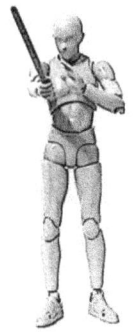
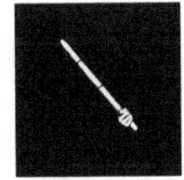

ARNIS

2. Backhand strike to *opponent's* right temple (*striker's* left side);

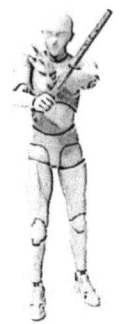
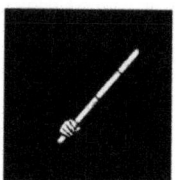

3. Forehand (*tigbis*) strike to opponent's right shoulder;

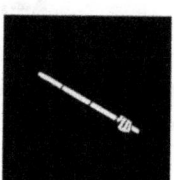

4. Backhand (*ordabis*) strike to opponent's left shoulder;

5. Thrust to opponent's solar plexus;

6. Overhand thrust to opponent's left upper chest;

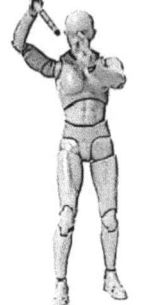
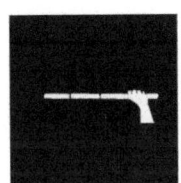

7. Overhand thrust to opponent's right upper chest;

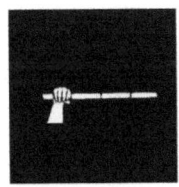

8. Backhand strike to opponent's right knee;

9. Forehand strike to opponent's left knee;

10. Overhand thrust to opponent's left eye;

  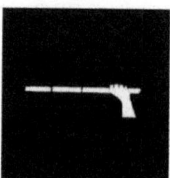

11. Overhand thrust to opponent's right eye;

12. Overhead strike to top of opponent's head.

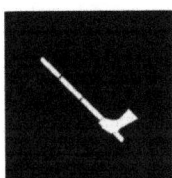

These are not the only strikes in Modern Arnis. For example, *witik* refers to a flicking strike commonly aimed at the opponent's wrist and a *salok* is an upward strike. These are, however, the fundamental twelve.

> **Leo Fong**, who learned stick-fighting from both Professor Presas and Angel Cabales of the Serrada Escrima tradition, practices a slightly different version of the Twelve Strikes, which includes attacks aimed at the wrist and groin. While striking the wrist may seem at odds with Modern Arnis's stick-on-stick innovation, when one considers the reason behind this principle—that striking stick-on-hand tends to cause injury—then including such techniques in the armamentarium of martial artist for use "in real," as opposed to practice settings, suddenly seems to make a lot of sense. Leo Fong's additional techniques can be practiced alongside the Modern Arnis core curriculum by simply adding three moves to the original twelve:

ARNIS

13. Underhand strike to opponent's groin (upward);

14. Forehand strike to opponent's left elbow/wrist;

  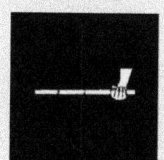

15. Backhand strike to opponent's left elbow/wrist.

⊗ **THIRD LESSON: CHOOSE YOUR TARGET.**

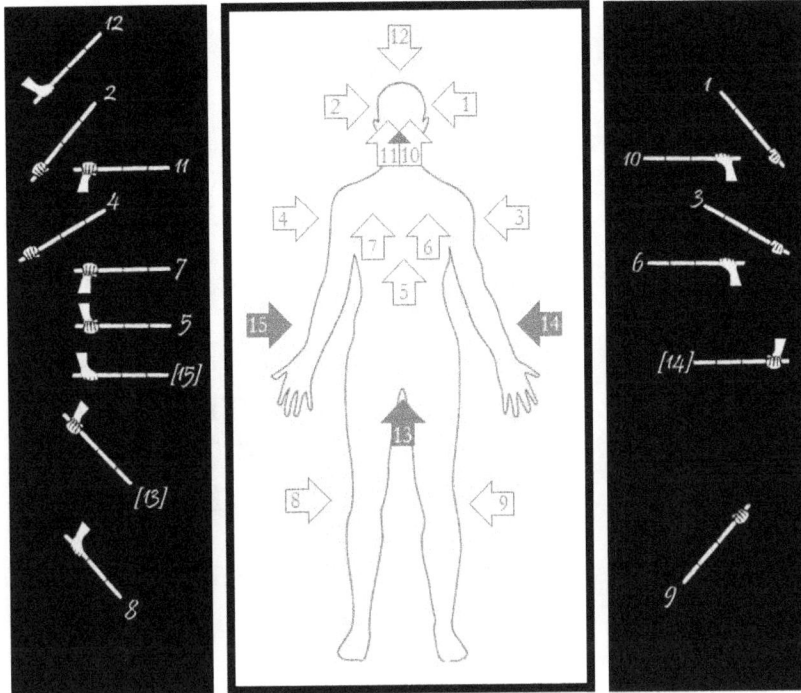

PRIMARY TARGETS

ARNIS

XIII. CHOOSE YOUR METHOD
I Will Show You How To Do It

MAKE IT SLOW...

There is a tendency for students who are new to a particular endeavor to seek to run before they can walk. The Professor was acutely aware of the bad habits this kind of rushed approach can breed, so he had a very simple maxim when teaching a new technique:

"First, make it slow..."

By explicitly telling his students to perform the move slowly in the beginning, he effortlessly removed any sense of pressure or competitiveness from the essential process of truly understanding what they were doing. Only once the technique had been properly absorbed would he challenge them to increase the pace to a realistic level *("...then, make it faster!")*.

> ⊗ **FOURTH LESSON: MAKE IT SLOW... THEN MAKE IT FASTER!**

STRIKING VERSUS CUTTING

The Professor would often use the terms 'strike' and 'slice' interchangeably. Just as he was equally comfortable fighting with either hand, he was able to transition effortlessly from a stick-based to a blade-based approach and back again. Novices, however, often fall victim to wielding the cane more like a club than a sword. Visualizing, or even practicing with, a sword from time-to-time will help to impress upon the practitioner the distinction between mere striking and *cutting* with the cane. Anyo Apat (Stick Form Four), for example, takes on a vastly different character when performed with a blade, or the image of one in mind.

> Tom Bolden draws students' attention to "the drip line"—a naturally-occurring, slightly raised ridge running the length of most rattan canes, which can be used to help visualize a cutting edge and orient the weapon accordingly...

STRIKE/CUT WITH EVERY MOVE

In David Mamet's play "Glengarry Glen Ross," Blake (the character played by Alec Baldwin in the film) tells his salesmen: "A-B-C, A-Always, B-Be, C-Closing, *always* be closing!" In this regard, the axiom of the arnisador, should be: "A-B-C, A-Always, B-Be, C-Cutting, *always* be cutting!" (but delivered in a much more gentlemanly way than Blake did). In other words, strive never to move the stick without striking or the blade without cutting.

> ⊗ **FIFTH LESSON: ALWAYS BE CUTTING/STRIKING.**

STRIKE WITH PURPOSE

There are many ways to strike with the cane. Some of the more common variations include:

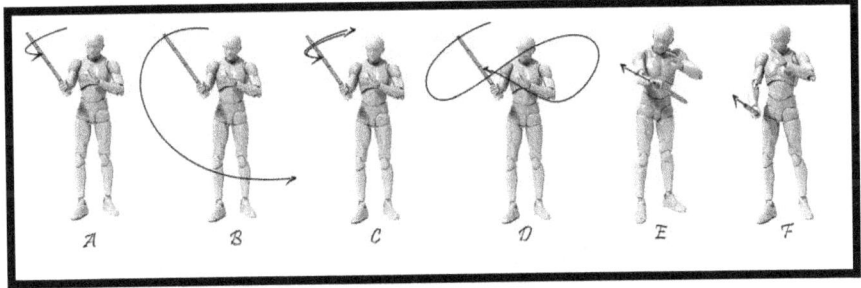

A. Striking/cutting **directly to the target**;

B. Striking/cutting with **follow-through**;

C. Striking/cutting with **retraction**;

D. Striking/cutting with **continuous flow**;

E. **Hammering/hooking** (with *punyo*);

F. **Thrusting** (with *punta*).

ARNIS

> **Doug Pierre** often teaches that each strike with the cane/blade should actually involve three strikes:
>
> 1. The first occurs during what is commonly assumed to be nothing more than the preparatory positioning of the weapon.
>
> 2. The second takes place during the strike itself.
>
> 3. The third happens during what is often called a mere retraction.

Each of these approaches has associated advantages and disadvantages. Follow through tends to be stronger but less controlled; retraction is often weaker but harder to trap; continuous flow is typically less powerful but more difficult to evade. Practitioners should be well versed in performing all the basic strikes using these various methods, and know when to employ each kind.

ED WALDICK 'FLOWING'

BASIC BLOCKING METHODS

Just as there are multiple ways of striking, there are also several ways to block. Critical to blocking with purpose is deciding whether the defender wishes to have the cane end up above or below the line of engagement, because this will dictate what follow-on options are available. Obtaining the preferred result generally depends on whether a "slice block" or a "cut block" is employed:

    A. **Slice blocks** glance off the target, generally remaining above the line of engagement;

    B. **Cut blocks** move through the target, generally ending up below the line of engagement;

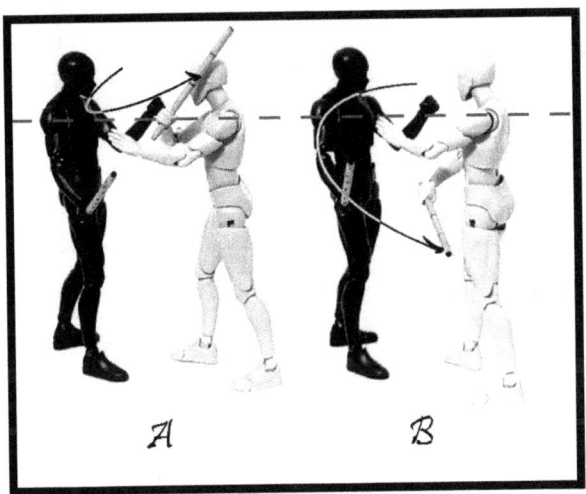

Ken Smith, once a butcher by trade, sometimes demonstrates the difference between 'slicing' and 'cutting' by running his blade along the forearm like this (it is a sensation which, once felt, is not easily forgotten!):

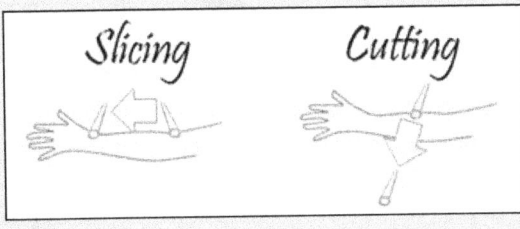

ARNIS

C. **Umbrella blocks** (*payong/sumbrada*) ward off an overhead attack with the live hand assisting;

D. **Wing blocks** also ward off an overhead attack, but the distinction is that the *punta* is generally aimed to the 'closed' (i.e. not 'open') side;

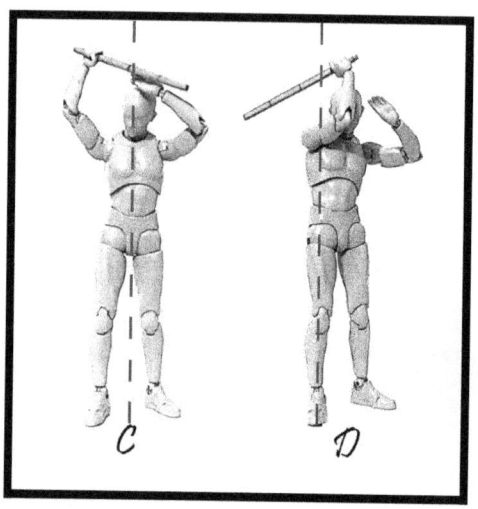

E. **Brace blocks** meet the opponent's cane with force. For this reason, the live hand is used to reinforce the technique, and to follow on with a disarm;

F. **Drop blocks** snap down sharply to deflect a weapon attacking along a low line, knocking it off course. It's a good idea to step back with this technique.

SIXTH LESSON: CUT/STRIKE/BLOCK WITH PURPOSE.

CLASSICAL STRIKING METHODS

There are many so-called "striking styles" in Arnis, which generally describe the pattern or shape made by the technique. The first three are **single cane, straight line** techniques (even though figure eights follow a curved path, the strikes themselves are along straight diagonal lines):

1. ***Banda y Banda***—The technical translation of which is 'belt-belt,' refers to a side-to-side striking pattern. In Cartesian terms, *banda y banda* moves mainly along the x-axis. It is important for students to learn to turn the cane when changing directions so that the leading edge is always 'cutting'. As with many—even most—Modern Arnis techniques, the live hand complements the movement of the weapon, typically tracking an equal and opposite path.

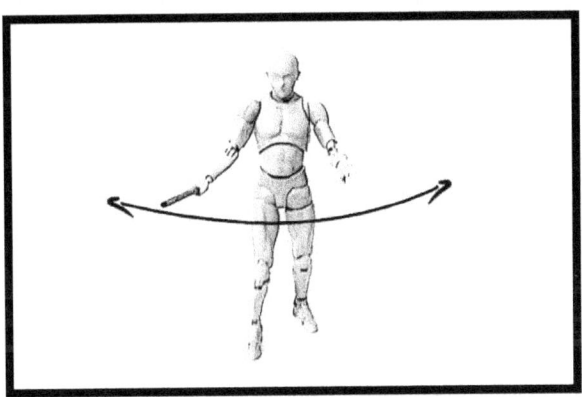

Banda y banda was often the first technique the Professor would teach new students. In addition to instilling in them the importance of the flow, it is also the principle with which he defeated five robbers who once attacked him at a subway station!

2. ***Rompida***—The technical translation of which is 'to break,' refers to an up-and-down striking pattern. In Cartesian terms, this technique moves primarily along the y-axis. As with *banda y banda*, in performing this method correctly it is important to 'cut,' and not merely lift the stick, on the upward part of the cycle. Keeping the *punyo* outside of the wrist throughout the process will assist in performing this technique in the correct manner.

ARNIS

> *Rompida* is a surprisingly effective technique when employed against a multitude of curved, flowing strikes. It quite literally cuts to the chase!

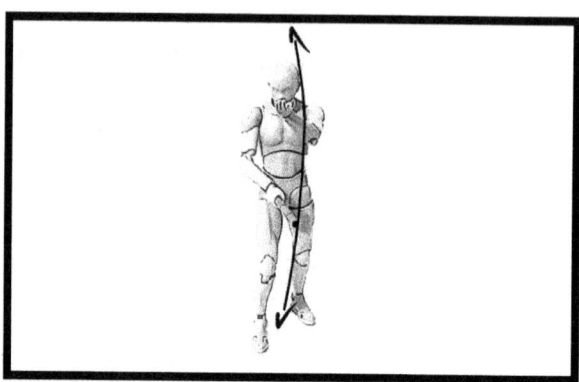

3. **Ocho-Ocho**—The technical translation of which is 'eight-eight,' refers to a continuous looping striking pattern in which the cane tracks the path of a figure eight on its side. In Cartesian terms, this method moves along both the x-axis and y-axis. While the pattern is curved, the strikes themselves are along relatively straight diagonal lines. When the direction of the cutting motion is downward, then it is a reverse figure eight.

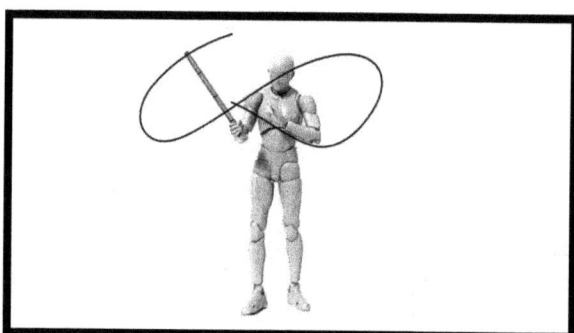

> Many blade arts categorize strikes using angles that roughly correspond to the points of a compass (meaning that on overhead strike would be 'north,' and a right diagonal strike would be 'northwest), and so on).
> By combining the angles of *banda-y-banda*, *rompida*, and *ocho-ocho*, the Modern Arnis practitioner covers all eight points of the compass.

The next three patterns involve **single cane, curving** techniques:

4. **Abanico**—The technical translation of which is 'fan,' refers to a

curved striking pattern in which the cane tracks arcs on either side of the hand. This can be employed along the x-axis, the y-axis, and even the z-axis (as with *abanico hirada*).

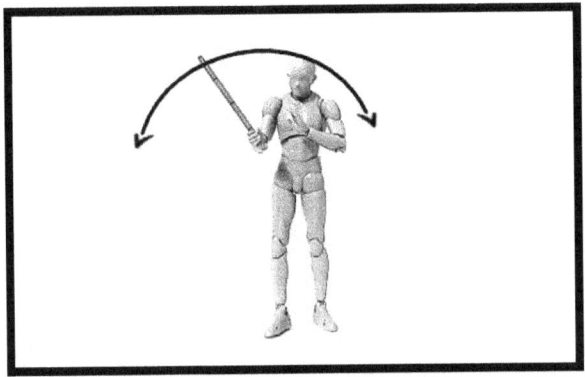

⊗ ABANICO DOBLE ACTION ⊗

Given the Professor's attitude toward training and teaching in general, it is not surprising that after learning *abanico* from his grandfather, he later invented a *doble action* (double action) variation on this method.

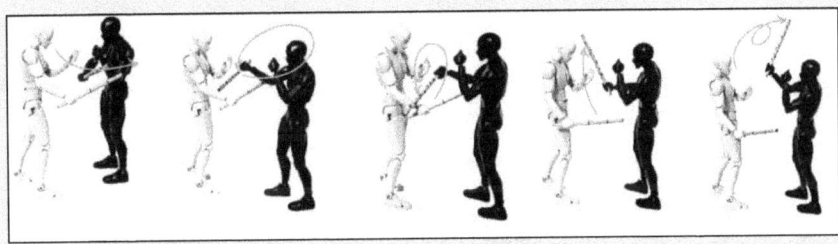

†— Strike with # 1 (right forehand to ⊕'s left temple);
⊕— Slice block, control with live hand;
⊕— Abanico strike clockwise to inside of †'s right wrist/cane;
⊕— Abanico strike counterclockwise to outside of †'s right wrist/cane;
⊕— First strike of Double Zero retraction (under †'s left elbow);
⊕— Second strike of Double Zero retraction (under †'s chin).

To the untrained eye, *abanico doble action* can look like a series of twirls and flourishes assembled for the sake of flashy appearance. To the initiated, however, nothing could be farther from the truth. In keeping with the Pierre doctrine, every motion is a cut. Practiced this way, the Professor's innovation becomes a furious flurry of slices that will quite simply overwhelm almost any defense.

5. ***Doble Zero***—Built into *abanico doble action* is the *doble zero* retraction. *Doble zero* strikes (or retractions) follow a looping path in order to facilitate hitting the same (or a similar) target twice.

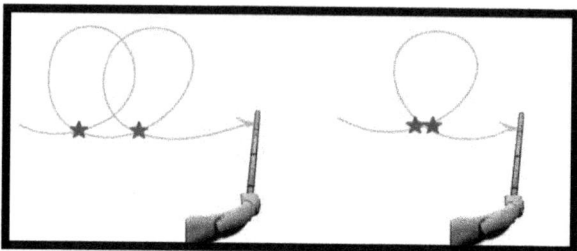

Often misunderstood, **Ken Smith** explains that the idea behind this technique is not that the practitioner makes two separate circles (pictured on the left), but rather that the practitioner makes *two* strikes (stars) in *one* circle (pictured on the right). This "second strike" technique can be practiced in any direction (vertically, horizontally, diagonally, forward...).

6. ***Palis-Palis***—The technical translation of which is 'sweep-sweep,' refers to a gently curving pattern which safely and effectively passes the opponent's strike. Strikes can be passed from side to side, from high to low, or a combination of these. So as to avoid having the force of the attacker' strike collapse the defender's grip, it is advisable to use the *debile* of the cane to make initial contact with the opponent's weapon.

Brian Zawilinski, a corrections officer with tremendous real world experience, indicates entry points for possible attacks by referencing the numbers on a clock face, and demonstrates how *palis-palis* can be used to redirect a strike from one such position to another.

GIVE-AND TAKE DRILLS

As with *abanico doble action*, once a basic technique or method is learned, it can be integrated with others and expanded to create an infinite armamentarium of permutations and combinations. Practicing these combinations with a partner is sometimes called a "give-and-take" drill in Modern Arnis. One commonly taught exercise of this nature is the six-count drill.

⊗ SIX COUNT DRILL ⊗
☥ — Strike with # 1 (right forehand to ⊕'s left temple);
⊕ — Cut block (end up below line of engagement), control with live hand;
⊕ — Counterstrike with # 8 (right backhand to ☥'s right knee);
☥ — Drop block (cane hand punches straight down, live hand controls);
☥ — Counterstrike with # 12 (right hand overhead to top of ⊕'s head);
⊕ — Umbrella block (overhead, live hand assists), counterstrike #1…

1

2

3

ARNIS

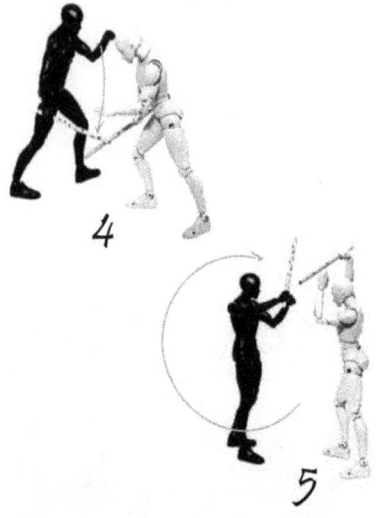

4

5

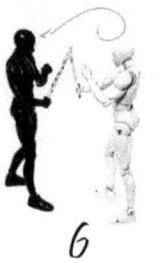

6

XIV. USE YOUR BODY
Body Shifting

In an art where lengths of hardwood and razor sharp blades are being swung at speeds approaching a hundred miles an hour, it is vital that practitioners learn not only to use their weapons effectively, but also to move their bodies.

> **Dan Inasanto**—direct student of the late Bruce Lee—prefers the name "Kali" for the Filipino stick-fighting art he teaches. According to Dan, the term is a portmanteau for the Cebuano words *"kamot"* (hand) and *"lihok"* (motion).

The importance of footwork in Modern Arnis cannot be overstated. In the competition between flesh and steel (or wood), steel (or wood) wins every time. As a result, the body must move to avoid or accommodate the weapon, not the other way around. A proper sense of this dynamic can be obtained by practicing with an armed opponent without having a defensive weapon, and therefore having to rely on dodging and ducking to avoid getting hit. And even when both practitioners are armed, the value of this approach should not be forgotten. In this regard, the Professor would often remind his student of the importance of "body sifting!"

> ⊗ **SEVENTH LESSON: SHIFT YOUR BODY WITH THE TECHNIQUE.**

THE V-STEP

One of the easiest ways to tell if students are new to the practice of Modern Arnis is to watch their feet. If they stay rooted to the floor during the execution of technique, their owners likely lack experience. If they flow with the moves, well then they probably know what burning rattan smells like!

The fundamental footwork of Modern Arnis is the V-step, so named because the practitioner's feet trace the letter "V" on the floor as it is performed. In a left foot forward fighting stance, for example, the lead foot is placed at the "top" of the left "arm" of the notional letter "V." When the practitioner decides to reorient to a right foot forward stance, he slides his rear/right foot forward so that it now rests at the "top" of the right "arm" of the letter "V," and slides the left foot back to the vertex of the notional letter. In so doing, the angle of his body will shift accordingly, like a swinging door. The feeling—and often the very purpose—of this move is avoiding a frontal attack.

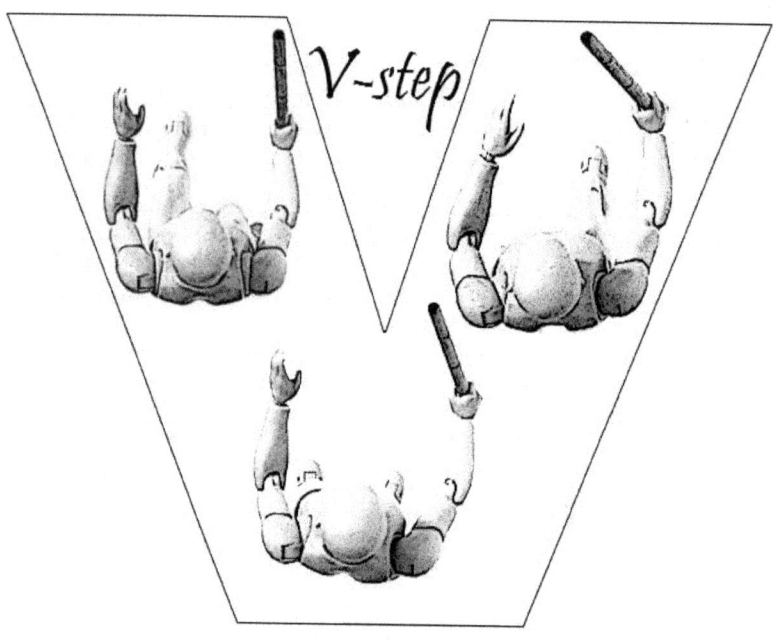

BANTAY KAMAY (THE "LIVE HAND")

One of the secrets to the Professor's amazing abilities was that even though he was functionally ambidextrous with the cane, he was in truth left handed. Since the vast majority of his students were right-handed, however, and many or most Arnis drills presuppose that both partners are working from the same side/hand, the Professor frequently sparred with the weapon in his non-dominant hand. For those who struggled to keep up with him even with this "home-court advantage," there was a pronounced sinking feeling when he shifted the cane to his dominant hand.

Regardless of which hand is holding the cane (assuming two canes are not being used), the other hand must remain alive and engaged as well. This aspect of Modern Arnis differs from such arts as fencing (in which the off-hand is hidden) for several reasons:

1. **Safety:** At a minimum, keeping the "live hand" engaged will serve to protect the face from accidental or deliberate contact.

2. **Balance:** Moving the "live hand" in counterpoint to the cane helps to balance the practitioner's movements and cover any defensive gaps.

3. **Utility:** Even though combatants may be armed, the utility of an open hand used alone or in combination with the weapon hand should not be overlooked. The "live hand" is a great close-range tool and can be used for trapping, locking, checking, disarming, striking, controlling, or supporting the weapon/weapon hand.

Arnis

> **Three Ranges**
>
> ⊗ *Largo*: Close enough to reach the opponent's stick only;
> ⊗ *Medio*: Close enough to reach the opponent's hand and stick;
> ⊗ *Corto*: Close enough to reach the opponent's body, hand and stick.

When engaging cane-against-cane, it is quite common to block or otherwise deflect the attacker's weapon with your own cane. Rather than viewing this as an impasse, keeping the "live hand" in mind encourages the combatant to look for opportunities to augment or extend the technique. Accordingly, the opponent may be disarmed, the defense may be strengthened, the adversary's free hand may be controlled, or a target may be struck, all using the "live hand."

> A wonderful piece of blade-fighting wisdom comes from **Dennis Tosten**: Whenever an opponent engages with you, you will find that you have access to at least one of the following:
>
> 1. The opponent's weapon;
> 2. Your own weapon;
> 3. Your opponent's hand;
> 4. A viable target.

KICKING

By extension, arnisadors should also take care not to forget the power of kicking (*sikaran*). While the "cane hand" may present a more obvious weapon than the "live hand," and the "live hand" may seem more readily available than the legs, the total warrior deploys all the weapons in the armamentarium in order to achieve victory on the battlefield.

ARNIS

XV. DOUBLE CANE (*DOBLE BASTON*)
Two Hands Are Better Than One

As legendary master swordsman Miyamoto Musashi discovered in the course of scores of duels-to-the-death in sixteenth century Japan, two swords are better than one.

In addition to doubling the number of weapons available to the practitioner, the use of two canes (*doble baston*), sword and dagger (*espada y daga*), or even a pair of palm sticks (*dulo-dulo*) are prime examples of the kind of two-handed practice that trains the student to use both hands, regardless of whether either is holding a weapon. This, in turn, fosters the kind of ambidexterity that made the Professor such a formidable fighter.

DOUBLE CANE/WEAPON STRIKING METHODS

There are several types of weapons, and methods for employing them **two-handed**, in Modern Arnis:

1. ***Sinawali***—The technical translation of which is 'weaving,' refers to a group of sinuous striking patterns that can be performed with two canes, one, or even none at all, making it in many ways the Rosetta Stone of Modern Arnis.

    A. **Single *Sinawali*, One Cane**—This method begin with a deceptively simple single-stick drill in which two partners strike cane-against-cane at a high level (≈#1) and continue along the same curved trajectory to strike cane-against-cane at a low level (≈#8), then reverse directions backtracking along the previous elliptical path to strike again at a high level (≈#2) continuing to culminate in a low level strike (≈#9).

B. **Single *Sinawali*, Two Canes**—The next level of this method involves achieving the same four-count, high-low-high, striking pattern, but using two canes. In this variation, the first two strikes (high level ≈#1 and low level ≈#8) are performed by both partners with the right stick, and the second two strikes (high level ≈#2 and low level strike ≈#9) are executed with the left hand.

C. **Double *Sinawali*, Two Canes**—The next step in this progression is a three-count, high-low-high variation in which the first strike is performed with the right hand (high level ≈#1), the second is performed with the left hand (left-handed low level, ≈#9), and the third returns to the right hand (high level ≈#2)

D. **Reverse *Sinawali*, Two Canes**—In the reverse version practitioners follow a three-count, low-low-low pattern as follows: the first strike is performed with the left hand (left-handed low level ≈#8), the second is performed with the right hand (low level ≈#9), and for the third, the left hand continues in its initial trajectory circling up and over to execute a second strike very much like the first (left-handed low level ≈#8)

E. **Empty Hand *Sinawali***—The empty hand translation of *sinawali* is easy to understand. Any of the drills described above can be performed using the palms (and occasionally the backs) of the hands. When performed with empty hands, the *sinawali* movement is an incredibly effective fighting technique. It has many valuable 'translations,' including circular blocking, trapping, and locking (standing center lock and bent-elbow wrist lock, to name just two).

Through this evolution, the value of Arnis's unconventional progression from *armed* to *unarmed* combat (as opposed to the more typical, reverse order) becomes very clear.

2. ***Redonda***—The technical translation of which is 'round,' refers to a striking pattern in which *two* canes make *three* strikes in rapid succession to *one* target. A helpful way to learn this technique, as well as to trace the origin of its name, is to perform strikes #1 and #3 by making a round "double zero" with one weapon, and then injecting strike #2 using the other hand/weapon in between. This technique, often practiced by having a partner hold a pair of sticks as targets at waist height, roughly parallel to the ground, teaches the practitioner to deliver a continuous flurry of blows that all but the most experienced fighters will have a great deal of trouble dealing with.

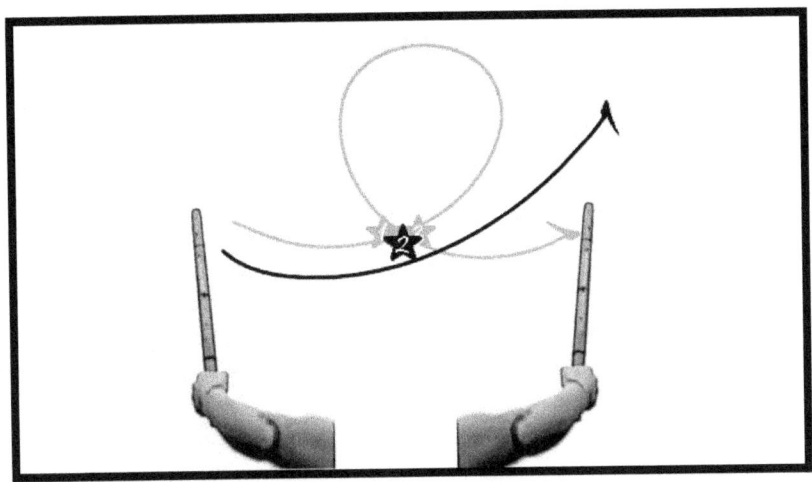

3. **Crossada**—The technical translation of which is 'crossing,' refers to a method in which the weapons in each hand cross (close) or uncross (open), thereby creating a scissoring movement ("*gunting*") on a target that is caught between them. *Crossada* style is generally performed along the "high line" or the "low line," depending on the position of the target, giving rise to four primary variations: *Crossada* can be performed with canes, blades, or even empty hands. Below it is illustrated using *espada y daga* (sword and dagger).

ARNIS

⊗ CROSSADA ⊗	OPENING (*Abierta*)	CLOSING (*Serrada*)
HIGH LINE	HIGH OPENING	HIGH CLOSING
LOW LINE	LOW OPENING	LOW CLOSING

[4.] ***Espada y Daga***—The technical translation of which is "sword and dagger," is not a particular pattern, but rather a way of performing many patterns using these two weapons. For example, many two cane styles (like *crossada*) can be performed using *espada y daga*, and vice versa. By this point, you should be hearing the Professor whispering in your ear: *"It is all the same, you know…"* However, when using the long and short blade, the dagger is primarily responsible for maneuvering and/or disarming the opponent, while the sword does the brunt of the passing. It is for this reason that the shorter weapon is usually held close to the body.

Daga **(Knife)**—Some FMA practitioners focus significantly, or even primarily, on the use of the short blade alone. Entire volumes could be written on this subject, but suffice it to say for present purposes that any well-rounded practitioner of Modern Arnis must have at least some familiarity with knife-fighting.

Bram Frank is an expert in the use of the knife/*bolo*, and his instruction in this discipline is sought out by private and public organizations around the world. His **Ten Commandments of Steel** are:

1. Steel cuts flesh, ***always***;

2. You cannot change Rule 1;

3. Unless you are wearing a blue suit with a big red "S" on the chest, Rules 1 and 2 apply;

4. The principle of the bladed tool—that an edge cuts flesh—has never changed;

5. Always lead with the edge and thrust with the point;

6. The proper grip is determined by range-to-target;

7. Disarming the opponent is an unrealistic goal;

> 8. Accessibility is paramount; no access, no weapon;
>
> 9. Using steel is a life-and-death situation;
>
> 10. In a knife-fight, when one person drips and the other gushes, that quickly turns into: one person gushes and the other wears a toe-tag.

[5.] ***Dulo-Dulo***—The technical translation of which is 'end-end,' refers to pairs of short palm sticks only a few inches in length. Like the Japanese Kubotan, Filipino *dulo-dulo* can be used to augment strikes and locks, to target pressure points, and to crush flesh. As a paired weapon, *dulo-dulo* also fit with the Modern Arnis principle of encouraging ambidextrous training and technique.

A few key principles for employing *dulo-dulo* effectively are:

    A. Just as the cane is an extension of the arm, *dulo-dulo* is an extension of the hand.

    B. Use the edges (and any sharp points) of *dulo-dulo* to strike pressure points.

    C. Use the length of *dulo-dulo* to apply pressure to flesh.

    D. Use the *punyo/punta* of *dulo-dulo* to assist with *buno* (locking).

ARNIS

E. Almost any short item can be used in this way (pen, keychain, even a cellphone).

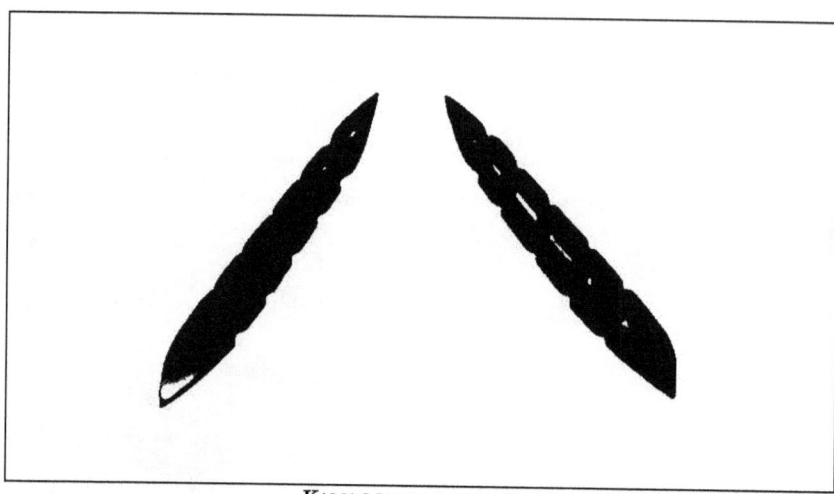

KAMAGONG DULO-DULO

XVI. EMPTY HAND
Arm Blades

The Philippines is often described as a "blade culture," in large part because knives are not only commonplace in these islands, but also because, at least until recently, they have been more typical street weapons than guns.ˣ As we have seen, it is from this blade culture that Modern Arnis arose. And like many styles of Filipino Martial Arts ("FMA"), arnisadors begin their training with cane in hand. All of this focus on the weapon sometimes distracts observers from the empty-handed aspects of the art.

Failing to tap the rich vein of empty-handed techniques in the Modern Arnis curriculum, however, is a mistake, even for those who already practice a style of unarmed self-defense and initially seek merely to add the weapons component of Modern Arnis to their existing curricula. Keeping in mind the many empty-handed arts that the Professor studied and subsequently added to the recipe of Modern Arnis—Filipino Dumog, Japanese Karate and Judo, and elements of Small Circle Jujitsu, Okinawan Ryukyu Kempo, and Chinese Wei Kuen Do—this should come as no surprise.

Modern Arnis employs strikes, kicks, grappling, locks, chokes, and throws similar to those seen in various other systems of self-defense, but it also has a wealth of unarmed combat methods all its own, including:

1. The *Bolo*—Similar to an uppercut in western boxing;

2. The *Yutak*—A diagonal stomping kick;

3. Brush-Hold-Strike/Throw—A block-check-counter combination;

ˣ *See* Appendix A: <u>Mga Karunungan sa Larong Anis</u> by Placido Yambao (1957).

4. Slap-off/Pull-off—A "removal" technique for a follow-on attack;

> **Ken Smith** has described the slap-off/pull-off drill as one of the core competencies required of any serious student of Modern Arnis.

5. *Tulak*—Pushing the opponent/trapping a limb;

6. *De Cadena*—The technical translation of which is "of chains," also known as "trapping hands." This is one of the most simple, yet powerful and effective techniques in the martial armamentarium of Modern Arnis.

⊗ *DE CADENA* (TRAPPING HANDS) ⊗

A: †strikes at ⊕'s right temple with a right backfist;
B: ⊕ parries (*pa'awas*) with near side open hand;
C: ⊕'s far side open hand takes over the parry;
C: ⊕'s near side fist counters with backfist to †'s right temple;
D: †parries ⊕'s backfist with near side open hand…

ARNIS

XVII. FORMS
Make The Translation

The practice of forms can be a contentious subject. Some think they do nothing to increase combat-effectiveness. Others maintain that they are essential, describing them as catalogues of practical self-defense techniques. And still others prize them for their non-combat value. In addition, the term "form" covers a wide variety of patterns, from the scores of precise moves that make up an Okinawan karate kata to the handful of smooth actions that are employed in performing a Jujutsu throw.

In terms of the FMA, some systems have forms while others do not. For Modern Arnis, the Professor developed and documented (at least[X]) four stick forms while in the Philippines and five empty hand patterns after coming to the United States. The suffix *"pamalo"* can be added to differentiate between armed and unarmed *"anyos"*.

EMPTY HAND	STICK FORM
ANYO ISA [A-1]	ANYO ISA (PAMALO) [P-1]
ANYO DALAWA [A-2]	ANYO DALAWA (PAMALO) [P-2]
ANYO TATLO [A-3]	ANYO TATLO (PAMALO) [P-3]
ANYO APAT [A-4]	ANYO APAT (PAMALO) [P-4]
ANYO LIMA [A-5]	

While the Modern Arnis forms have a decidedly Filipino flavor, their footwork often parallels the familiar I-formation or K-formation commonly seen in Japanese/Okinawan kata (A-1, A-2, A-3, A-4, and P-4). Those that do not fit this mold tend to employ footwork that is much more expansive in both the horizontal and vertical planes (P-2, P-3). And virtually all of the Anyos feature fast, flowing, frequently-florid hand-movements.

[X] The Professor endorsed several additional open hand forms during his lifetime.

ANYO APAT (PAMALO)—STICK FORM FOUR

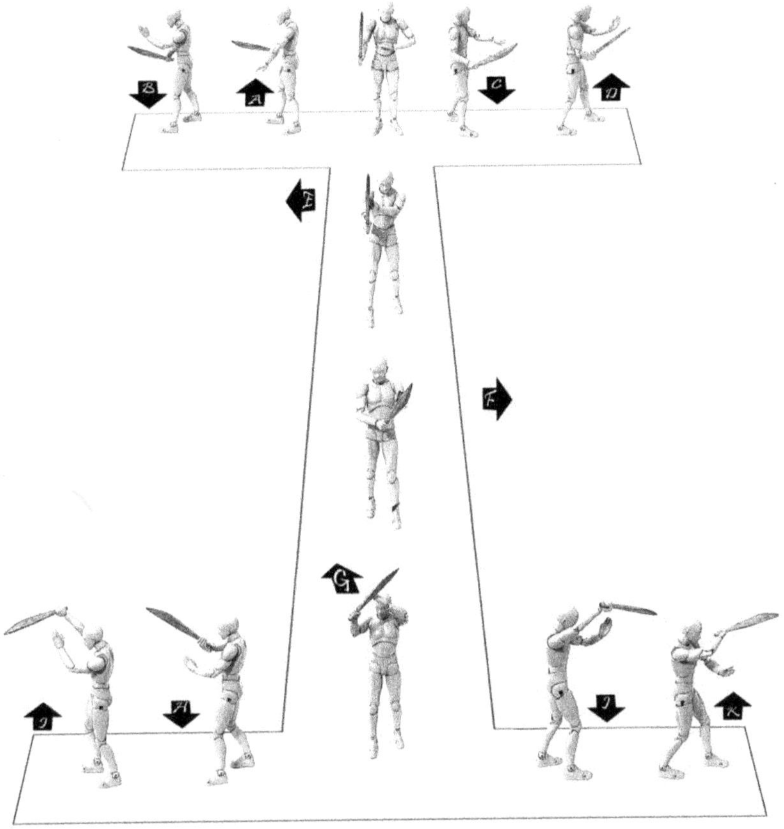

A. TURN RIGHT 90 DEGREES & CUT DOWN LEFT DIAGONAL;
B. STEP FORWARD LEFT & CUT DOWN RIGHT DIAGONAL;
C. TURN RIGHT 180 (OUTSIDE) & CUT DOWN LEFT DIAGONAL;
D. STEP FORWARD LEFT & CUT DOWN RIGHT DIAGONAL;
E. TURN RIGHT 90 & BRACE BLOCK RIGHT;
F. STEP FORWARD LEFT & BRACE BLOCK LEFT;
G. STEP FORWARD RIGHT & OVERHEAD UMBRELLA BLOCK;
H. TURN LEFT 270 & CUT RISING RIGHT DIAGONAL (*SABOY*);
I. STEP FORWARD RIGHT & CUT RISING LEFT DIAGONAL;
J. TURN RIGHT 180 & CUT RISING LEFT DIAGONAL;
K. STEP FORWARD LEFT & CUT RISING RIGHT DIAGONAL;

Arnis

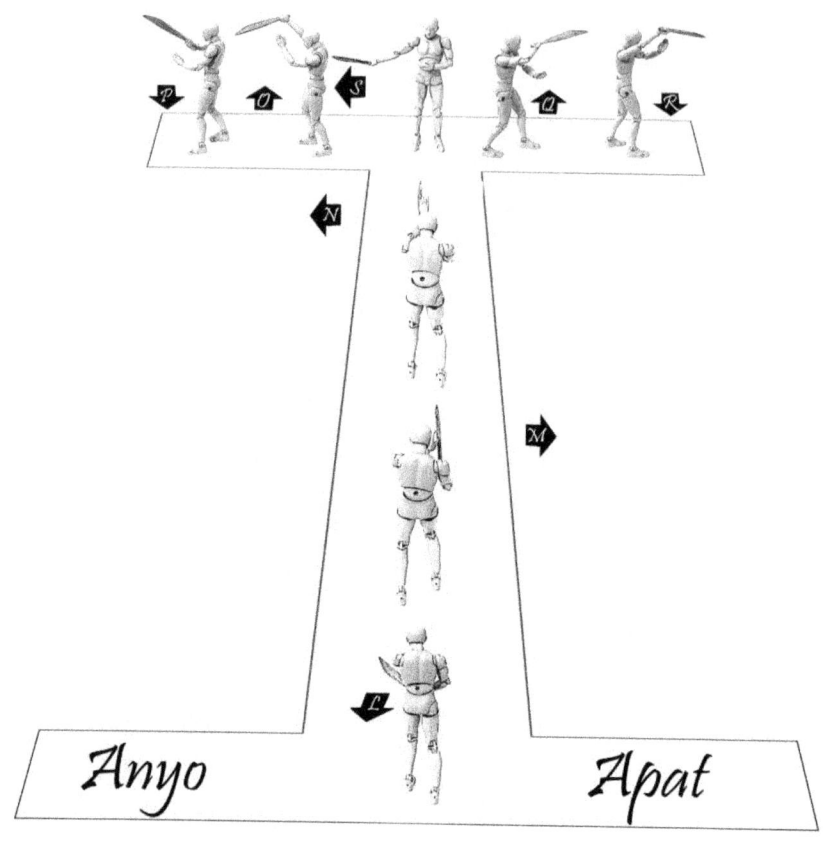

L. Turn left 90 & cut down right diagonal;
M. Step forward right & right brace block;
N. Step forward left & left brace block;
O. Turn right 270 & cut left rising diagonal;
P. Step forward left & cut right rising diagonal;
Q. Turn right 180 (outside) & left rising diagonal;
R. Step forward left & cut right rising diagonal;
S. Turn right 90 (front) & cut out to the right side.

As discussed, one of the Professor's favorite directives to students was, *"Make it slow."* This is especially useful advice in the practice of forms, where the idea is to absorb the deep meaning of the pattern through patient practice and painstaking polishing, not merely to memorize its superficial motions for just long enough to move on to the next one. *"Make it slow,"* he would tell students, and once they had done that properly, only then would he invite them to *"make is faster!"*

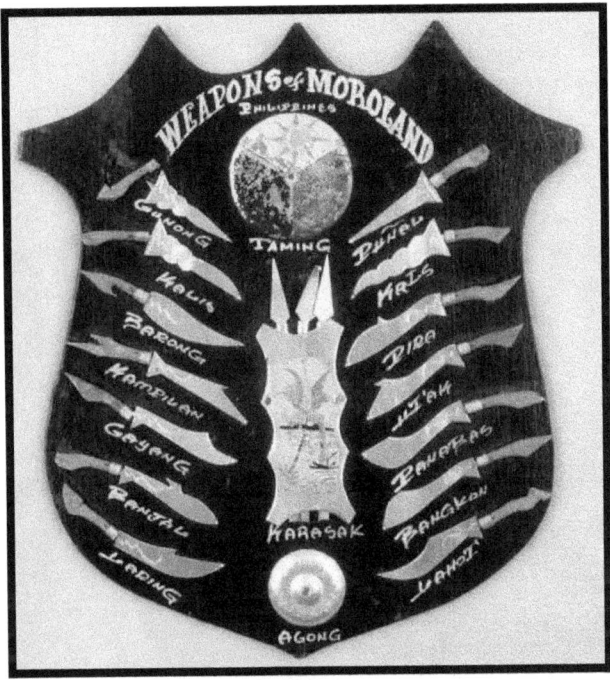

ARNIS

XVIII. THE FLOW
You Have It Already!

If there was one saying, one teaching, of the Professor's that eclipsed all others it was this: *"You must have the flow."* The Flow. So much is contained in these seven letters…

The Flow of Technique: First there is the idea of fundamental fluidity of movement. Modern Arnis is certainly a flowing art. Each move naturally runs into the next, and there are very few "corners" in which to trap a skilled practitioner or "edges" to grasp hold of. And when the Professor was your partner (which privilege he shared out liberally) it was sometimes more of a riptide than a flow!

The Flow of Practice: Second, when arnisadors find themselves deeply immersed in give-and-take drills, the flow of that practice is often faster than conscious thought can process, requiring them to run on instinct rather than deliberation. This forces them into what Leo Fong describes as, "the Zen Zone"; a perfect mindset (or perhaps no-mindset) for the development of martial expertise.

The Flow of Time: Third, all martial arts are handed down from master to student in a temporal tide that originates in the mists of antiquity and disappears over the distant horizon into the future. This might be thought of as, "the Universal Flow." As soon as you pick up a stick, you are caught in its current. In pursuit of this Flow, it may help to keep another of the Professor's favorite sayings—favorite teachings—in mind: *"You have it already!"*

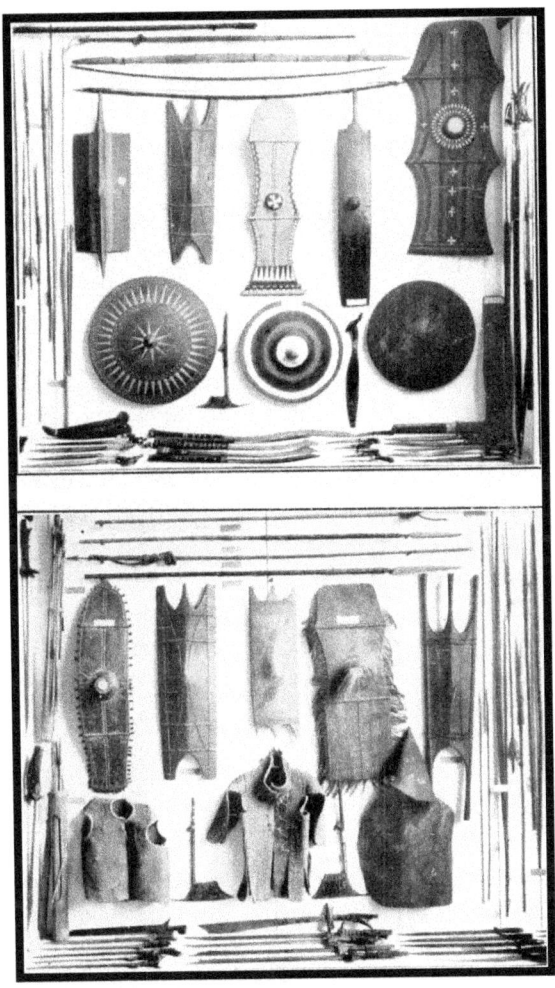

ARNIS

IXX. FRIENDS, FAMILY, AND FOLLOWERS
You Are Part Of My Family Now...

This work is the product of the collaborative efforts of many of Professor Presas' friends, family, and followers. It is for this reason that authorship is credited to *Mag Aaral* (not a person, but rather the Tagalog word for "student").

WHAT'S IN A NAME?

As previously discussed, Remy Amador Presas earned the title of "Professor" early on in life, in both the academic and the martial realms. Over the years that followed, some still called him "Remy;" others referred to him as, "Grandmaster Presas," and still others, "Professor Presas." But to many of his senior students who knew him well, he was simply "Professor" (no definite article).

The giving of a special name can serve to strengthen the bond between people in many ways. So it was with Professor. And it is fitting that he—who loved to give nicknames to his students—became widely known by this simple moniker. However, throughout this text, including the submissions that follow, the more conventional pattern of using the definite article before the title (i.e. "<u>the</u> Professor") is employed in the interests of consistency and readability for the uninitiated.

In addition to setting down the story of the master and his art, it was the Editors' goal to bring together in this work as many of the divergent branches which sprang from the common root of the Professor's art as possible. The number and diversity of the submissions that follow is truly a testament to his legacy. Here, then, in their own voices, are the memories of those who knew him best:

♦ JANET AALFS ♦

I was a relatively new black belt in Shuri-ryu Okinawan Karate (received from Grandmaster Robert Trias and Sensei Wendi Dragonfire in 1980) when I met Professor Presas at a 1981 Modern Arnis seminar in Connecticut organized by Sensei Dragonfire and Valley Women's Martial Arts. She had trained with the Professor on the west coast, felt the magic, and wanted others to experience his gifts. At that fateful seminar that initiated the spread of Modern Arnis to the east coast, I immediately connected with the rhythm, joy, challenge, sweat, puzzle-forming, knot-making, collaborative weave of the figure-eight, and the phenomenal skill and enthusiasm with which the Professor presented his art. I picked up a pair of canes, and have never put them down, incredibly grateful that I keep feeling the Professor's generous spirit guiding my work. Salamatpo!

The deepest and most lasting joys that I continue to receive from studying with the Professor include:

⊗ All the amazing, kind, skillful, trustworthy people I've had the pleasure of meeting over the years, and with whom I continue to connect, learn from, teach, exchange techniques and laughs and serious business.

⊗ The concept and practice of Arnis as "the art within your art," and how everyone brings her or his own special flavors from other arts. This depth of learning through cultural exchange has in all directions expanded and strengthened my understanding and application of these movement languages. It underscores what I believe the core of this practice is about: martial=power within; arts=creative energy; martial arts=directing energy in life-enhancing ways. As I like to say, "Martial arts has ART in it twice!"

⊗ Following the figure-eight pattern of infinity. That there is always so much more to learn keeps me hungry, humble, grateful to be alive, curious, and inspired to be even more kind toward myself and others as we strive to be the best we can be. This partner and group work keeps giving me the next opportunity to observe that excellence arises from how we cooperate.

ARNIS

You-I-We. Unity strengthens, diversity transforms. Our differences may cause painful stuck places at times, but ultimately if we are paying attention, these highly charged points give us energy to do the next creative and inclusive thing – Courage!

♦ DAN ANDERSON ♦

I first met the Professor through a friend of mine—Fred King—at a tournament in Oakland, California in 1979 (at a time when his Modern Arnis was still pre-Tapi-Tapi and included more of the Presas family system). Fred was always trying to introduce me to experts from other systems of martial arts, but since I was competing and winning sparring tournaments on the national level at the time, I just wasn't interested. Fred was all afire about this new master he'd met: Professor Remy Presas. All I knew was that this "Professor" guy was tagging along with Fred at the tournament. Fred even had him staying in the same hotel room as us. At first, I was just hoping we could rid of him!

I woke up at six the next morning to the sound of *"pat-pat-pat, pat-pat-pat, pat-pat-pat"*—the Professor and Fred were practicing trapping hands in the room! I said, "Guys, come on, it's six o'clock in the morning, give me a break!" Then there was silence. And about an hour later, from a distance, I heard, *"clack-clack-clack, clack-clack-clack, clack-clack-clack"*—they were doing Sinawali out in the parking lot! And I thought, "these guys are nuts!"

Later that day, during some downtime between the elimination rounds of the tournament and the finals, the Professor started telling me about a time that he had been jumped by a couple of guys in New York City. I swear he must have seen me rolling my eyes. He told me that one of them had grabbed him by the wrist, and he invited me to try doing so the same way. Then he did a very simple walk-through move. I had seen this move many times before in other arts, but the way in which he did it hit me like a ton of bricks. I had fought with competitors of all sorts, with all levels of confidence, but the manner in which the Professor performed this technique was beyond confident—there wasn't a thought in his mind that it might not work. And at that exact moment, "the top of my head blew off" and my attitude changed completely. My first thought was, "I've really gotta watch this guy!"

About six months later, another instructor had the Professor in for a seminar which I attended, and I was *captivated*. I immediately saw the Modern Arnis was "the missing piece of the pie." I had been trained in what was essentially a karate system—all kick and punch. There was zero weapons work, zero joint-locking, and zero throwing. None. What I was missing most was a transition from being a "karate jock" into becoming a martial artist. A huge part of what came from Modern Arnis was the Flow.

> ### The Flow
>
> The Flow is the basis of Modern Arnis, but the Flow is not *a* drill; it's a concept that has **many** drills that develop it. The Flow is like a stream—never stuck in one place, but rather flowing over, under, and around everything in its path. If you get too caught up in a given technique, you lose your connection with your opponent, and tend to miss what's right in front of you. As the Professor used to say: *"Do not become hypnotized by the stick."* If you drill the technique to the point that it becomes instinctive, this does not happen.

That's when I started adopting Arnis into what I was doing. The amazing part is that if the Professor hadn't been patient with this cocky karate guy, and waited for me to see the light, it might never have happened. And Modern Arnis was a huge part of my development as a martial artist.

One thing to keep in mind about the Professor is that notwithstanding how much he smiled, and how generous he was, the man was a fighter. His training in the Presas family style and the Balintawak style made him a tough fighter. Fred King and I gravitated more toward the fighting aspect of his system (as opposed to artistic expression). And there is no doubt in my mind that it is a combat-effective system, as evidenced by its use by people like myself (a tournament fighter), Chuck Gauss (a police officer), Brian Zawilinski (a corrections officer), Kelly Worden, and Bram Frank (both well-known knife experts).

> ### Just What I Needed
>
> As he got older, it seemed to me that the Professor's focus shifted to teaching upper body motion as opposed to lower body motion. I initially assumed that it was because he wasn't as agile as he used to be. It was only later that I realized that the truth was that his angles had become so perfect that he needed to do less and less. You can see the same thing in tapes of Wally Jay as he got older. These guys had their systems down to a pinpoint degree of accuracy—not a sixteenth of an inch was wasted!
>
> I have found through research that as the masters got older, their movements minimized to exactly what they needed to do and no more. I have found myself following this same path. My footwork used to be more expansive in the beginning. Now it has shortened up a bit to accommodate what is needed and wanted in any move I do. Professors Presas and Jay, as well as Manong Ted Buot (my Balintawak teacher) are terrific role models to emulate.

I love all of the art of Modern Arnis, but there are two things that really stood out from the beginning for me:

⊗ The first was the Professor's disarms. One moment you had your stick, then he got hold of it, and suddenly you didn't have the stick anymore! And it wasn't based on strength or ballistic speed. This fascinated me, so I made a study of it, in order to try to achieve the same level of *effortlessness*.

⊗ The second thing was how well he moved for such an "old guy" (he was 45 years of age at the time. I am now 64. That thought makes me laugh...)! The Flow of Modern Arnis instilled a fluidity in him that kept him young. This same flow is what I try to emulate with my actions.

> ### The "Kenny Rogers" Rule
>
> I have a number of "rules" for combat that I title humorously to make them easy to remember. One of these is the "Kenny Rogers Rule." If my opponent is executing a disarm on me, I don't tug and jerk against that physical contact. More often than not, the opponent's move will give me access to another target. When you are connected with your opponent, it always presents you with some kind of opportunity. I refer to this ability to flow with the progression techniques as: "The Kenny Rogers Rule"— ♪ *You got to know when to hold 'em...* ♪

These days I teach my own brand of Modern Arnis: The MA80 System Arnis/Eskrima. I don't always do exactly what the Professor—or any other teacher—did in performing my technique. Rather, I try to replicate the *manner* in which he executed his techniques. If your body isn't the same shape, or your muscles aren't the same size, as your teacher, you're going to have a hard time doing things exactly the same way, so the idea is to figure out the principles and concepts underlying those techniques. None of us who were long-term students of Professor Presas are physically built the same as him, nor have we had the same life experiences. A key point the Professor made over the years was to *make this art our own*. I think this has been all of his senior students' homework since his passing. It certainly has been mine.

> ### GUTEI'S FINGER
>
> A student once asked master Gutei what made the tide come in and go out. In response, Gutei simply pointed at the moon. Later, the student told his friends that his master had shown him the secret of the tides. "What is it!?" they asked. "His *finger*," the student replied!

I continue to work on becoming as well-rounded an arnis/eskrima player as possible. Here is a concept I apply very heavily in my arnis training: Back when I fought in karate tournaments, I noticed that many competitors were unable to deal with surprises. If they didn't train a particular move, they'd get hit by it. It's the "left turn at Albuquerque"—the unexpected move—that gets you every time. I do the same with my personal arnis training. There are two definitions of the "MA" in the MA80 System Arnis/Eskrima. One is obviously "Modern Arnis," but the other is "Masid Arnis" (*"masid"* means "study or research of...").

Masid Arnis is "Dan Arnis." It is my own research and development. My concept is: "If you have experience at everything, you'll be surprised by nothing." It is my goal to make sure that I have seen and done as much of everything as possible; to avoid being surprised. This encapsulates something that the Professor said to me many years ago, which became one of the four pillars of my system: *"Danny, if you can counter, you will not be beaten!"* Thank you Sir—working on it...

ARNIS

♦ DR. JEROME BARBER ♦

I first met Remy in Buffalo, New York, in the early 80s. My instructor at that time was Don Zanghi—he was Remy's Western New York representative at that time—and had brought the Professor in to teach a seminar. Between his accent, and my knowing almost nothing about the stick at the time, I could not follow his movements at all. So I put the cane in my left hand, and followed his movements that way.

> **MIRROR IMAGES**
> Remy was *left*-handed, but usually demonstrated with his *right* for the convenience of his students, so when Dr. Barber mirror-imaged the movements with his *left* hand, he was inadvertently mimicking the Professor's dominant side).

Remy saw this and came over to me on a break and asked if I was left-handed. I said "no" and explained, and he said, "Very good! You will be very good because you can train both left and right!"

As I came to know Remy, I remember him telling me "You must learn this art because it is from your people." I thought to myself, "Is he crazy? My people are here in America and over in Africa, but not in the Philippines!" But when I began looking into it, I came to understand that there were people of color in the Philippines known as "Negritos," and I found this fascinating! Apparently, they followed the land bridge out of Africa and across India, and then rigged up rafts to come and settle the island of Negros. Their use of bow-and-arrows speaks to this ancient connection. In fact, in the one of his videos, Remy performs the fourth stick form using a Negrito-style bolo sword (which I have adopted as a symbol of my art). It took me some time to see the connection between

Kenpo and Arnis, but when I finally did, I knew that I wanted to study both

> **SOFTLY, SOFTLY**
> Some of my favorite techniques involve the softer approach to fighting. For example, I love to train and teach Palis-Palis—double stick or even empty hand—because it involves *passing* the force rather than meeting it head-on.

During the Professor's lifetime, Modern Arnis headquarters was wherever Remy was. Since his passing I don't think the Modern Arnis community will ever be united under a single banner again, but I agree with and support the Editors efforts to try to bring people a little closer together in this book. In 2003, I put together a symposium in with that same idea in mind—to give people an opportunity to meet one another face-to-face, and even hash out any differences they might have had—and I think it was moderately successful.

> **THE DIZZY GILLESPIE RULE**
> In my art, I follow the "Dizzy Gillespie Rule"—When I see something I like, I *steal* it and make it my own. But I never forget where it came from and I always give credit....

One of the achievement I am most proud of is creating the first and only U.S. college-based training program to feature Modern Arnis. Founded at Erie Community College in Orchard Park, New York, this program (the Kenpo-Arnis Self Defense Program) awards academic credit to students upon successful completion. I taught the program from 1987 until 2012, at which time two of my students took over and continue to teach it to this day. In April 1989, with the assistance of two students, I had the opportunity to demonstrate every technique in the curriculum to the Professor, who approved and gave his blessing to the program. In 1992, Grandmasters Tom Bolden and Al Tracy added their approval to the Professor's.

ARNIS

♦ MICHAEL BATES ♦

My story concerning Professor Presas begins at the end of his life. In the fall of 2000, I attended the Professor's Camp in Chicago. While there, we discussed his upcoming tour of Europe and North Africa, the Tenth Annual Fall Seminar which I regularly hosted in Media, and what was to be his first ever Winter Camp, set to take place in Philadelphia the following February.

While in Hamburg, however, the Professor became very ill and needed emergency surgery. Many of his senior students flew to Germany to be by his side. Unfortunately, I was not able to get through to him at the time to discuss how this might impact the many plans we had discussed, but he subsequently reached out to me and told me to go ahead with the Fall seminar, and that he would come to Winter Camp, where we could discuss what he had in mind for the future of the organization.

The Professor called me many times from his home in Canada over the weeks that followed, and told me how important it was to him to make the trip to Philadelphia, but by the time the Winter Camp began, with the better part of a hundred people in attendance, I thought that there was only about a ten percent chance that he would be able to attend.

In the middle of this event, however, my cell rang. It was the Professor asking me to pick him up at the airport. When I saw him, the horseshoe scar on his skull told the horrific story of his battle. To think he flew from another country, in his weakened condition, to support his art and plan its future boggles my mind to this day...

He had no bags and no medication. Luckily I had a bunch of cash to give him! We made our way slowly to the car and then back to the venue. When he entered the four thousand foot training area, people literally gasped in surprise. "Continue" he said. And they did, after taking many,

many pictures. He stayed for two weeks after the seminar before having to return to Canada for a medical follow-up.

During this final visit, we talked about many things, among them, his plans for the Modern Arnis Hall of Fame Foundation. Tragically, he was never able to return, as we had discussed, to finalize these plans, but in the years since his passing, I have done my best to honor his wishes in this regard to the best of my understanding and ability.

THE MODERN ARNIS HALL OF FAME FOUNDATION

On the tenth anniversary of Professor Presas' passing, Michael Bates decided that the climate might finally be right to establish the foundation that he and the Professor had discussed in the months leading up to the final seminar in February 2001. **The Modern Arnis Hall of Fame Foundation**, which nominates practitioners who have made significant contributions to the art for induction into its ranks, now holds annual seminars at Villanova University every summer. Fundamental to this organization is the principle that *all who practice Modern Arnis are welcome*. Inductees and instructors have been drawn from almost every branch of the art, and profits are routinely donated to worthy causes.

ARNIS

♦ Tom Bolden ♦

In the 1960s I served in the U.S. Marine Corps. In the summer of 1964 I was transferred to a camp in Hawaii. While there, I trained at a Kenpo school on Oahu, and one of my Filipino instructors—Master Florentino Pancipanci—introduced me to stick-fighting. He demonstrated this art using rolled up newspapers! At first I didn't even know what it was...

A few months before I left the service, I moved back to the mainland, and even after leaving the Corps and joining IBM as an Engineer, I continued to study and teach martial arts (Kenpo Karate, Aikido, Tai Chi, Tae Kwon Do, Kung Fu, and Capoeira), but it wasn't until 1984 that I met Grandmaster Remy Presas. I went to a seminar at Rosemont College in Pennsylvania, and as soon as I walked up to the desk to register, Remy came up and introduced himself. I remember thinking, "What a friendly guy!"

I noticed right away that what he was teaching was a little different from what I had initially learned—it was more karate-based—but I was able to adapt. It was a two week camp, we trained until late into the night, and it was hot—almost unbearable! After that, Remy ran many camps in my area (New York, New Hampshire) and I never missed one.

PRACTICE MAKES PERFECT

One of my favorite techniques is Abanico Double Action—one of the Professor's innovations. When I first saw it, I loved it, so I went and practiced it—a lot! At camps, the Professor would often ask me to demonstrate this technique in particular. He would say, "Make it beautiful!"

In time, I came to recognize the influence of Escrima on Kenpo. I learned so much from Remy about how to translate from stick to empty hand technique. In my current training, I incorporate aspects of many arts—I also used to study dance as well—and the more I studied, the more I came to realize that the body only does so many things (or as Remy would say, "It is all the same!").

◊ **Dr. Tye Botting** ◊

Photo by Bob Hubbard
BOBHUBBARDPHOTOGRAPHY.COM

I started my Modern Arnis training under Guro Eric Alexander in 1991, but it wasn't until 1993 that I first met the Professor at a Camp in Dallas. He used me as his 'dummy' at that event, and as soon as we crossed hands, I was completely hooked! There are many ways to get to the top of the mountain, and I recognized instantly that his was one that I wanted to follow. It was totally unexpected, but it filled hole that I didn't know I had...

Breaking It Down

There are some things I didn't quite get when the Professor first showed them. I would try to deconstruct and reconstruct them, going back to their roots, to develop understanding. Sometimes it just takes some time for things to 'ferment.'

After that first meeting, I trained with him as often as I could, and I relished being his 'dummy' because I learned a lot that way. While I couldn't always *see* exactly what he was doing from that position, I could certainly *feel* it. I would often go back and ask other students what it looked like, and once they described it to me, I could work it effectively because I knew what it was supposed to feel like.

Arnis

> ## Kung Fu Roots
>
> I think that training in Kung Fu helped me get the most out of Modern Arnis, and vice versa. I already had pretty good flow and relaxation, and that helped me to 'chain' things together when I began training in Modern Arnis. In both arts, I strive to strike as effectively as possible with the least amount of effort. So they meshed really well (for me at least).

You knew you were doing okay if you could get the Professor to switch to using his left (dominant) hand. I remember one particular seminar where Eric was doing a knife drill with the Professor. They were going really fast, and Eric seemed to be holding his own—but just barely. Eventually everyone gathered around to watch. At that point, something changed, and suddenly Eric was getting beaten pretty handily. We then realized that he had made the Professor switch to his "good hand," so we all gave him a pat on the back afterwards!

> ## Internal Energy
>
> The Professor had a great deal of internal strength, which not many appreciated at the time. By touching him, you could feel it—his efficiency, his connection to the ground, his structure, his sensitivity, and the power that comes from all of that—so whenever he taught something that synced along those lines with me, I grabbed onto that in a heartbeat and used it. I don't know that he gave this to me on purpose, but I really enjoy that aspect of the art.

I look back on the time when the Professor first started introducing Tapi-Tapi to his Texas students. He began by teaching me the left side. He pushed me and pushed me to the point that I thought to myself, "Man, I'm moving really fast – this is awesome!" But now when I look back on the tape of that class, I cringe because I look so slow and clunky on the film! To me, the Abecedario are the baby steps, the basics, for all that makes up Tapi-Tapi.

I don't like to use the term "bait" because it tends to make people skimp on what should be a proper technique. In other words, what people sometimes call the "bait" should ideally be a full-strength strike, and if it happens to be blocked, then there is a follow-up. Either way, as the Professor used to say, "I hit you anyway!" I consider that phrase a great one-liner for the sum of his teaching.

> ### THE BIG PICTURE
>
> Some of my favorite techniques were the ones the Professor shared on the spur of the moment, because they were often the ones that he didn't show to everybody. I try to train with other Modern Arnis students—people I consider from my relatives in the Professor's family—from every branch of his art because each of us has things that the others may not have seen before, and I have had pretty good experiences in this regard. When we come together and share those techniques now, we all get to see more of the Professor than we otherwise would have.
>
> I think that it's a mistake to focus on only one aspect of the art, because it's a complete system, and if people focus on only one area, they are missing the bigger picture, not only for themselves, but also for the next person they share it with.

Another time, the Professor and I were doing some hard, fast, broken rhythm, give-and-take drills. When working with the Professor, you knew that every move could be a finishing technique, but that he was letting the drill flow along. At one point, I blocked a strike, but apparently not well enough, because my own cane popped back and hit me in the head! The Professor looked so concerned and apologized, even though it was my fault. I knew it was an occupational hazard, but it was really touching to see that he cared about his students so much…

> ### THE THIRD HAND
>
> Sometimes, the Professor would release a trapped hand, but at the same time, close the distance and press his belly against that hand, thereby creating pressure and the *physical illusion* that the trapped hand was still being held, even if only for a moment. I think of this as "the third hand."

Looking back on the early days, I remember that the Professor always stressed the importance of having **fun** in training. In fact, during my first Camp, I was training with a bunch of friends who were real cut-ups, and Eric told us more than once that maybe it looked like we were having *too much* fun! The way the testing at the end worked out said a lot about the Professor: We thought we were testing for a beginner rank of some kind. Based on our performance, however, the Board recommended us to go straight to black. But the Professor said, "But I do not know them!" He didn't know us at that point and couldn't tell whether we would be dedicated to the art, but at the same time, he recognized our pre-existing

ARNIS

abilities and the recommendation of the Board. In the end, he split the difference and approved us to go to one of the mid-level ranks. This was definitely the right thing to do, and was just another example of his wisdom in my opinion.

The Professor had a great way of remembering people and adopting them into his martial family. When I would show up unexpectedly at seminars from time-to-time, he would always stop what he was doing and shout out: *"Da Tye!"* He made me feel so welcome—I felt like he was my martial grandfather, and I still miss him…

FILIPINO WARRIORS

◊ Bruce Chiu ◊

In 1982, I read an article about Professor Remy Presas in *Black Belt* magazine. I was so impressed by what he was doing—integrating his art into other arts—that I dropped out of college and went to go and try to find him in North Hollywood, where he was teaching at the time!

The Basics

The Professor often told me that Trapping Hands, Single Sinawali, and the Six-Count Drill were the three most important things to practice. During the years between our first meeting and our second, I didn't know too much, so I practiced what I *did* know over and over again, and, as a result, I got pretty good at it.

After that first encounter, I went some time before seeing him again. In the early 90s, I went to one of his seminars in St. Petersburg, Florida. I was waiting in the lobby of the venue for him to arrive, and the moment he walked in, his eyes lit up, and he came over and greeted me by name. He was amazing that way. A lot of folks recognize that he was a master of the martial arts. What few understand is that he was also a master of *people*.

The School of Hard Knocks

Never forget: The Professor came from a hard tradition. When he took his shirt off, you could see the scars on his back. The Philippines was a dangerous place when he was learning his art. For example, there was a particular arnisador at that time from political powerful family who would challenge other fighters, and if they won, his bodyguard would shoot them! The Professor knew it was only a matter of time until he found himself facing this no-win scenario, so he got out ahead of it by going to the other man and asking to be his student. By the second day of training together, the man recognized that Remy was the better fighter.

After our second meeting, I couldn't catch up to him—it was like trying to catch the wind! But this time, I was in a better place in my life, so I was able to latch onto him and follow him wherever he went. I think I did 48 seminars in one year at some point! Jeff Faulkner and I put a **lot** of miles on his beat-up old Isuzu pickup. After one particular three-day camp, I had to drive home using my forearms on the steering wheel because my wrists and fingers were out of commission!

THE VIEW FROM DOWN HERE!

One of my favorite techniques is a disarm from a forehand strike. It took me *forever* to learn because he did it so fast, and a lot of the time, I was the one he was doing it on (it was sometimes hard—in more ways than one—being the Professor's uke, but it was an honor that I truly cherish. I learned a lot from "looking up!"). I would ask some of the other guys how to do it afterwards, and it became a standing joke that they wouldn't tell me! Eventually I was able to learn it. There's also a step-through throw that I love. It's an old, old technique that I initially had trouble remembering, but now it's among my favorites.

One of the things the Professor did was teach me how to *teach* (not just how to do techniques). He taught me how put on seminars and how to deal with people. He told me to partner up with Leon Jay and Jack Hogan. He was very good to me that way. He allowed me to sell his products as well, and, apart from his videotapes, he always let me keep the proceeds of those sales. It was one of his many gifts to me…

YOU HAVE IT ALREADY!

The Professor often said that the highest form of the art was "no weapon". Students would sometimes ask, "When am I going to learn double cane?" "When am I going to learn the knife?" And I would laugh, because the amazing thing about this system is that they *already knew it*— they just didn't *know* that they knew it. If you can do it with empty-handed, you can do it with the stick, and vice versa. So if anyone out there regrets that the Professor didn't get a chance to teach them some aspect of the art, take heart: Maybe he did teach it to you after all…

At one particular seminar in Gainesville, Florida, the Professor had me in a lock, and the butt of his cane was just resting on my gallbladder points. He said, "This could be knockout—but that is Dillman's business, and I did not take the class to wake them up!" Then he tapped me and I was <u>done</u>. There were mats on the floor everywhere except for one little area. Now the Professor didn't like to stand on pads, so guess where I dropped…

> **IN REAL**
>
> His economy of motion and efficiency of action were unparalleled. Once we were practicing a drill together and I asked him if he would use it in a combat situation. "Oh no," he replied, "I would do this; attack me again." I came blasting in and he blocked my strike with his left hand, grabbed my throat with his right, swept my legs, took me down, and hit the ground by my head so close that it brushed my hair. I was never been more scared in my life. "*That* is what I would do if it was real."

1999 was a tough year for me health-wise. When I was in the hospital, the Professor came to visit me and sat up with me all night. It was one of the most remarkable things that I've ever experienced. For a while after leaving the hospital, he was very protective of me. At one point, he forgot and we started sparring at a seminar—it was fantastic—but as soon as he remembered, he made us stop.

> **YOU ARE DEAD NOW!**
>
> The Professor was an *amazing* fighter. I remember sparring with him once using as much speed and power as I had. Sweat and blood were dripping off me. He was hitting my knuckles one at a time, in order, with abanico strikes. And all the while *he was watching TV!* I remember it was during the Clinton impeachment hearings, and he kept saying, "Oh, Clinton is in trouble..." Well I was young and dumb at the time, and thought I saw an opening. I remember thinking to myself, "I got him this time." But as I raised the stick to go for the 'kill-shot,' I realized that he had intentionally maneuvered me right under the ceiling fan in the room. Just then, the spinning blades disarmed me! He smiled and said: "You are dead now!"

The Professor was a bit of a gypsy—always moving around. I asked him once why he didn't have a school, and he told me that it was because it would limit the number of people he could touch with art. He had a large number of post office boxes, and more ID cards than I've ever seen in one place! One thing that his senior students all know is that he had this great big suitcase full of who-knows-what that he wanted at every seminar. It was the senior students' responsibility to hand it off to one another as he traveled from place to place. Some of them became good friends of mine. I've been blessed in my life to work with very good people in my life, and my time and training with the Professor had a huge impact on me, both personally and professionally. I miss him every day...

ARNIS

♦ CHAD DULIN ♦

PHOTO BY BOB HUBBARD
BOBHUBBARDPHOTOGRAPHY.COM

I can't tell you where I first met Remy Presas. It was the early 90s, and it was at one of his seminars. That really means nothing, as he taught, on average, two or three seminars a week, probably forty-five weeks a year. The remaining weeks were reserved for longer camps, and the major holiday weekends, which even die-hard martial artists reserved for their families. He taught two techniques, or perhaps I should say I *remember* two of the techniques he taught. More experienced students realized that almost everything he did was a lesson in technique, or in application.

At first glance Professor Presas was an unremarkable man, but then you noticed his intensity. When he took the floor, one of his gifts became apparent: only rarely would he fail to connect with every last person in the room. As he began to teach and demonstrate, passion crackled like electricity. As he became more and more excited, words could not keep pace. Then he would slow down and calmly explain where the rest of us were to begin. He would ask as a favor: "Can you do this?"

Like many martial artists who came up in the 1980s, my first introduction to the Filipino Martial Arts was through Dan Inosanto's aptly named book: "The Filipino Martial Arts." My careworn edition has been with me for decades, and is worth far more to me than the inflated price it would bring on eBay. One cannot, however, learn new concepts of motion from a book, and Professor's first lesson was quite a revelation for me: "First," he said, "have two sticks. We will learn the Redonda!"

Double stick work is one of many core elements in the Filipino fighting arts, but it is a relatively minor element in Modern Arnis. The double stick translates well to the empty hand, and that was the first thing that would jump out at me. The Redonda, as taught, is nothing more than three chained strikes coming from the same direction. Done as a drill, it is three strikes delivered from the right, followed by three from the left—nothing amazing, but oh, that morning it was amazing... Still sunk very deep in my Korean martial roots, the looping re-chamber that fed the third strike in the series was like seeing color TV for the first time (yes, I am *that* old!). The possibilities!!

This was vintage Professor with a new student (me!). I left that day feeling a personal connection (and one would actually develop soon enough as I began following Professor around the South, and later the East), having a rudimentary new set of movement skills that I could teach to my students, and new insight into a combative movement set. I have attended longer seminars and walked away with far less!

But let us not forget the second technique embedded in my memory; one which ultimately had more real-world value. Professor also knew when to change gears as his audience began to fade. At some point he called for a break and asked us to return with only one stick (single stick is the more common training mode). Now, one needs to understand that English was not Professor's first language. Some of my seniors speculate that is was perhaps his fourth or fifth. One also needs also to understand that the "P" and "F" sounds are rather fluid, and in some cases interchangeable in various Filipino dialects.

Professor called us in close, and motioned for everyone to have a seat. Holding his single rattan stick he spoke softly, almost conspiratorially: "Sometimes, they will grab your cane… then you must *funish* them!" And the senior student there that day (and I am not sure who it may have been) was, indeed, *punished*. It was, Professor showed, a simple matter to pin the aggressor's hand to the stick, and then, with a simple twirl apply, what he termed "center lock" (martial arts terminology is enough to give anyone fits—center lock in Modern Arnis corresponds to *nikkyo* in the Japanese arts, or bent elbow wrist lock in Small Circle Jujitsu…). Suffice it to say that center lock is exquisitely painful when properly applied <u>un</u>assisted, and the addition of a twenty-some inch lever makes it that much more so!

There is nothing really special to this technique—it is similar to the basic baton retention methods taught at police academies across the country—but the devil is in the details. By changing it from a release to a "punishment"—by not allowing the aggressor to release—we end up with a powerful control technique. Remy Presas accomplished two things with me that day: he changed my concept of how attacks may be linked together so that they flow, and he whetted my appetite to learn more. He did the latter so well that to this day, my core art remains Presas Arnis. Oh, and there is a third thing: he gave me a technique that actually worked out "in the world" exactly as taught.

Some years later (I believe post 9/11, and therefore after Remy passed away), I had occasion to take a gentleman into custody who was heavily under the influence of PCP. I had been working uniformed patrol for several years and had seen quite a bit, but, being told to go perform an anatomically improbably act on myself by a man I was holding at gunpoint—that was a new experience... As the situation developed, it devolved into a baton encounter. Sure enough, sometimes they will indeed grab your stick. And I swear I heard that voice from the past in my ear: "You must *funish* them!"

It has now been fifteen years since Remy Presas passed away. Many of us strive to keep his art alive and growing, and I think we are succeeding in that there is a whole generation of students who have come into the art in the intervening years. I recently had a student at a camp express awe that I had trained with both Professor Presas and Professor Jay. In fact, that is part of the motivation for setting these stories down on paper. Many of us "old timers" recall Remy's use of language fondly, and we often quote him to one another as a way of sharing these memories and easing a loss that still stings. As you read these, well, "Remy-isms," understand that they are intended to convey the moment, and to remind my brothers and sisters in the art of days past. There is no mockery intended—just a sense of respect and loss.

◊ ANDY "TATTOO" FILARDO ◊

I started training with the Professor in the early 1980s at the Rosemont College Camp hosted by Joe Bridenstein; the camps in those days were two weeks long, so you got pretty good immersion! I had started in USA Goju, then shifted into boxing and kickboxing. When I met the Professor, I was fighting as an amateur out of Gleason's gym. Those camps were something—I remember being up at midnight comparing sidekicks with Randi Shea!

Arnis helped me as a competitor with my footwork, without a doubt. My coaches saw the change and said, "Wow—you are moving so much better!" Having people like Mike Morton swing for real forced me to learn angular footwork. In boxing, it was easier, more compact. The only difference is that Arnis changes the lead. Boxing is still a sport—a contact sport—but still a sport. If boxing/kickboxing is 'high school,' then Arnis is 'college.' It goes through every possibility.

FOUNDATIONS

My empty hand Arnis is very heavily influenced by Western boxing. There are many contradictions between art and fighting you see: Block-and-check becomes block-and-hit or block-and-slice. These are the basic keys to seeing the technique within the technique. You learn to do more with less; it really is the same thing. You start to focus on knowing just a few techniques.

The basic tools—body English; regular defenses; only sitting down on a punch when you can really hurt; moving on the balls of the feet; and the big three—conditioning, conditioning, and conditioning—that is what makes a fighter. That is what formed my Arnis! Conditioning teaches the mind to take the body where it doesn't want to go. That is where you discover a lot about yourself and your techniques. If I didn't believe it, I wouldn't do it. I am on a path that is true to me. I am not saying I know it all, but step up and test yourself! You can't prepare for combat by training the art.

My best training with the Professor happened while driving him around the northeast and off-the-mat training in hotel rooms. He knew I was a fighter and he respected that, but it wasn't always what he wanted in the seminars. One day, some guys had done a demonstration, and the Professor said, "That is good," but then he called me: "Tattoo!" He whispered, "We will show them!" He was pushing, but you could just flow and he would ride with whatever you gave him. At one point he disarmed me, and hit me with a punyo in the head. My head started bleeding, so I stepped off the mat and one of my guys handed me a rag. The Professor was still looking for someone else to work with when I jumped back up and we kept flowing. Finally he grabbed me and said, "*Now* we are done!"

> **KEEP IT SIMPLE!**
>
> In my method (the MFA method), we concentrate on single stick and empty hand. I didn't want to try to remember everything; I designed my system to be easy to remember. You learn the sequences as a way to understand the method and the concept. The mentality is to hit—combative mentality—but you have to adapt this mentality to the particular situation. If you are attacked you have many options—too many options. In a fight, you don't have time to go through all the options; you have to deal with the reality and be in the moment.

The real guys, the old time fighters, didn't have time for so many techniques. They had to inflict maximum damage with minimum effort. They were after the easiest way to inflict maximum damage. Combat is the father. The art was born from combat. Once it is watered down, there is no intent, no consequence. The combat element melts away. How do you know you can *fight*, if you never fight? The *real* contact stick fighting is how you discover *a lot* about yourself, real fighting, and what really works! You bring this knowledge back to your drills and training. Pain is a great teacher!

FILIPINO WARRIOR

♦ BRAM FRANK ♦

The bladed aspect of the art of Modern Arnis often goes unseen. On occasion, people will see what I do and ask, "Is that really Modern Arnis?" I think they sometimes focus on the stick aspect of the art so much that they forget that the Presas family was known for teaching the *bolo* (properly classified as a long knife as opposed to a short sword) to soldiers during the Second World War. It is important not to forget that edged weapons practice is at the very heart of this art.

> ### A BLADE ART
>
> Many years ago Professor Remy Presas talked to me of his father, uncle, and grandfather teaching bolo to the Filipino troops. He said he and his cousin Cristino would hide in the bushes and watch. Then they would go back to the yard by the house and use branches from the trees to mimic the actions being taught. One day, Remy's grandfather caught them and proceeded to teach them what he and Cristino called the Presas family style of bolo.

Because of the tactical and technical differences bewteen an edged weapon and a cane, Remy told me that I had to pick: either the stick or the blade. Not both, not a little of each but pick one. I love blades and I was scared to insult him, but I knew I had to do Presas family style bolo. When I told him my choice, he laughed and hugged me. The stick is the beauty of the art and the blade is the soul of the art. They are, as he showed me, similar, but different, and they have some things in common, but are subtly different. I can still hear him saying: "Bram, remember, the blade will make you honest, you cannot cheat or you will be cut!"

Arnis

Even though impact weapons and bladed tools are in many ways at opposite ends of the spectrum in terms of form and function, it is axiomatic in Modern Arnis that when students are working with sticks, they should envisage an 'edge' on the cane and align it with their second knuckles so that it is always pointed forwards in their grip.

> **ROMPIDA VERSUS UP-DOWN**
>
> One of the primary differences between Rompida and Up-Down is that in the former, the cane is turned when transitioning from downstroke to upstroke (and vice versa) so that its 'edge' is always facing the direction of travel, whereas in the latter, the grip—and by association, the orientation of the cane—does not change.

It is important to remember to switch mindset when transitioning from wood to steel in training, because many techniques that require grabbing the cane with the live hand or using some other body part to trap or manipulate it, could be fatal if employed against an edged weapon. There are also few—I any—second chances when fighting with steel. As a result, your techniques need to be simple, swift, and sure.

Remy knew and approved of my focus on edged weapons and their importance in his family's art. I think that is why he entrusted me with the Presas family bolos and the legacy that comes with this honor.

⊗ EIGHTH LESSON: STICK TEACHES KNIFE, KNIFE TEACHES HAND.

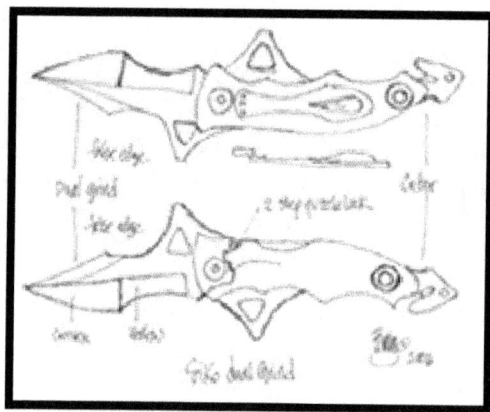

ONE OF BRAM'S DESIGNS

◊ Ray Goss ◊

One thing I remember is that Remy had a way of always making you feel special. He would walk up to me from time-to-time, seemingly at random (not as part of the class) and say, "I have something to show you." Then he would demonstrate something novel or intricate, or show me a new twist on a technique that I hadn't seen before. The amazing thing was that he had the ability to make everyone feel this way. And he did it both on and off the mat. For example, at a seminar in Texas many years ago, Remy was sitting in the corner of the room talking with some senior students when my wife and I walked into the room. I overheard him say to them, "Oh, these are my very good friends. Ah, from Pennsylvania. I am happy."

Another aspect of Remy's teaching style was that almost everyone he taught came away with a different perspective on the art. This might have been frustrating for those who wanted a more definitive syllabus, but I find it fascinating, and I think it showed the diversity of both Remy and his students. By avoiding rigidity, he was able to tailor his teaching to individual students, helping them to expand their knowledge and understanding, even of their other martial art systems. And by focusing on the individual student in this way, he made everyone feel welcome and valued.

Arnis

◊ Tim Hartman ◊

Photo by Bob Hubbard
BOBHUBBARDPHOTOGRAPHY.COM

I wanted to train in martial arts ever since I was little, watching *kung fu* theater with my dad. Fast forward to the 1980s and I was training informally with a bunch of my friends who are martial artists—doing the back yard/fight club thing. I was hanging out with some pretty serious martial artists at that time. We would spar and so on—I often didn't win, but I earned their respect. I had some skills, but I needed direction.

There was a local Isshin Ryu club in the area run by a guy named Bill Adams. Some of my friends trained there, and I decided that I would join if I didn't find something better by the end of the year. One day, a friend said to me "You've gotta come over to this place." This place—Filipino Karate Academy—was run by a man named John Bryant. I went, and they put a stick in my hand on the first day, and that was *that*. I knew right away that it was the form of expression for me. Even then I used to talk about the flow of life, about going with the flow of things.

Once I got my black belt, I spread out and started looking at the martial DNA of Modern Arnis. I wanted to know the 'whys;' that *this* came from *this*, and *that* came from *that*. And the Professor encouraged my individuality. There is the martial *system* (Modern Arnis) and then there is the martial *style* (interpretation). The Professor encouraged me to express my style.

Manong Ted Buot

One day we were at my house and Remy called Ted Buot. When got off the phone, he told me, "You will train with Ted." Ted and I had met before, but the Professor was the one who gave me the final push through

> the door. Remy said, "He will teach you to be a *real* stick fighter." I thought this was funny, especially after hearing stories of Remy's exploits from Manong Ted, because there was no question that Remy was a real stick fighter!

Because of my subsequent cross training in other Filipino Martial Arts, I now have an eclectic system. I started training in Balintawak Eskrima (the final system Remy Presas studied prior to forming Modern Arnis) in 2000 while the Professor was still healthy.

INFLUENCES

Modern Arnis was very heavily influenced by Balintawak. It is the foundation of the art. There is also a lot of Small Circle Jujitsu, which I completely embrace. Everything works on Wally Jay's two-way action, from disarms to grappling to striking. Wally and Remy were close friends, and constantly inspired one another; they were always evolving and growing.

Professor Presas often promoted Modern Arnis as, "the art within your art," essentially characterizing it as a cross-training discipline so that other instructors could import some Filipino-flavored self-defense into their schools, and established martial artists could expand their skill sets without abandoning the base arts in which they had invested years or decades. But there is another approach to this art, in which it is the core, stand-alone system, rather than a secondary endeavor.

I see my contribution to the art being the introduction of structure, from working with the Professor to organize camp tests in the early days to developing the comprehensive curriculum we now use in the WMAA. The martial arts should be an educational system, like a college program, where the student is exposed to, and ultimately draws upon, different specialty areas. Seniority matters, but so does proficiency; just like in college. The full-time student will accumulate material faster than a part-timer.

THE BROTHERS PRESAS

All three of the Presas brothers are world-class martial artists. Ernesto's Kombatan is essentially built on the same chassis as Modern Arnis, but has a very well-developed double stick program as its trademark. Roberto, the youngest (and only living) brother has developed *espada y daga* (sword or stick and dagger) as a specialty.

ARNIS

My intent is to pursue further integration of Roberto's art in the future. My vision of Arnis continues to evolve, pulling elements from the family art as expressed by all three brothers, continued study of Balintawak, and interaction with other, high level practitioners, both at home and abroad.

We refer to "Presas Arnis" to honor the contributions of all the family members, all the pieces that are integrated. It is common to hear people today speak of "combat proven" arts but we can't forget that Jose Presas was training resistance fighters during WWII; that the Presas family has a battlefield lineage. Dan Inosanto has the largest JKD organization in the world. People go to train with him because of who he is. Remy had that same attraction. When he first started teaching, the art was still called "escrima," and it was his wife who suggested using the term "arnis" so he would be different.

A style is only as good as the people doing it. Modern Arnis may not always have been the premier art in the Philippines or elsewhere, but Remy was undoubtedly the premier teacher. This is legacy that we need to build on.

FILIPINO WARRIORS

◊ WILL HIGGINBOTHAM ◊

George Dillman told me: "If you haven't trained under Remy Presas, you need to check him out. If you walk into a room holding a stick and he's there holding one too, you lay yours down and pay attention to what he's saying. He knows what he's talking about." So starting in about 1987, I took that advice and pretty soon I was hooked. I fell in love with that art as well and it became another component of my studies. While Remy was alive, he advised me to bring Chuck Gauss in for seminars in our area if we wanted to learn more between visits with him. So Chuck came to Indianapolis for me several times and when Remy died, I stayed tight with him and also developed a close relationship with Ken Smith.

*****

After one of the "Big Three" camps in Jacksonville, Florida, hosted by Jack Hogan, several of us were sitting having breakfast when we decided to go down to Saint Augustine for the day. We all loaded into cars and were following Jack who, was hauling the Dillmans. I had gone to that camp with my old friend, Jim Corn, who had taken his wife Janna's new Chevy Blazer for the trip. Remy hopped into the back seat and Jim had me do the driving while he sat in the passenger seat.

We were trying our best to keep up with Jack while the three of us were having fun talking and pointing out the sights. Then, Remy saw a big billboard of a reptile exhibit. He said, "Jim Corn, ALLIGATOR!" and grabbed Jim's side below his ribs with his left hand as if he were being attacked by an alligator. Jim flexed every muscle in his body and straightened up striking the roof of the Blazer with his head, hard and loud. If we had been in a convertible, I believe he would have launched himself right out of the car!

ARNIS

Remy and I starting laughing so hard I thought I was going to have to pull over because my eyes were watering. Then Jim, who was actually in pain, started laughing too. That evening when we returned to the hotel, Jim had a six inch diameter bruise on his side where Remy's "alligator" had bitten him. That was just his sense of humor...

*****

During one of the Michigan camps back when Terry Wareham hosted them, Remy was teaching a technique with an uke from Buffalo while we all sat watching. During the execution of the technique, the Professor struck his uke on the neck and he passed out.

> ### THE ART WITHIN YOUR ART (AND MINE)
>
> I remember once demonstrating a knockout technique for Remy using a move from a form in his own system: Anyo Dalawa. He was very pleased with this interpretation. He always encouraged students to put their own spin on his material.

It surprised Remy, who was now holding his uke up to keep him from falling. He said, "Where is Willie? Because if Willie do, Willie knockout!" He was referring to me because he had seen me do pressure point knockouts before. He slowly sat his uke down and selected someone else to demonstrate on. Remy, Wally and George often used things that they learned from each other while sharing.

FILIPINO WARRIORS

◊ Shishir Inocalla ◊

I first met Grandmaster Remy Presas at a tournament in 1982. I had been training in the martial arts for many years at that time, and I thought that I was already an expert. I was doing a demonstration at the tournament, and, after watching it, Grandmaster Presas said to me: *"You are very good, young man [anak]!"* I then realized that I was like a blade of grass in the garden, and that I could learn so much from him. We were together ever after that. I took him to Vancouver with me, and from then on, he pretty much adopted me and trained me, and made me the representative for Modern Arnis in Canada.

Weapon of Choice

One of my favorite weapons is the Filipino *balisong* (butterfly knife), and Grandmaster Presas helped me with writing Veintenueve Balisong: Filipino Knife Fighting in the early 1980s.

In the early 1970s, I was featured in an issue of *Black Belt* magazine. That led to being scouted as a film actor. I was fortunate to be cast in many movies and TV shows, often in Vancouver—the Hollywood of the North—and the Professor and I choreographed stunts for many scenes. Many people, especially young people, know me as Michelangelo from the *Ninja Turtles*. While my career in film prevented me from following the Professor for a while, it also opened many doors for me, especially in spreading the arts to young people.

A Complete Art

My favorite aspect of Modern Arnis is empty hand translations. Modern Arnis is a complete art—trapping, locking, striking, throwing—not just a stick-fighting art, and students must be able to understand the unarmed applications of the movements of bladed weapon.

As a child, I was a somewhat troubled kid, fighting in the streets here and there. I was referred to a Yoga teacher, and the study of this art helped to calm me down. At the age of twelve I was sent to India to study with a Yoga master. Two years later I became the first Filipino Yoga teacher to be certified in this way, and I left India to teach this art. When I returned many years later to visit my Yoga master, I was arrested and put in jail because the government of India disagreed with my teacher's political views. This experience tested me mentally and spiritually as well as physically.

One of the Professor's greatest strengths was his spirit. That is what made his so powerful, and able to overcome all the odds he faced. He was able to balance the internal and external aspects of the martial arts…

MIND, BODY, AND SPIRIT

One of the most important aspects of martial arts training is maintaining a balance of mind, body, and spirit. I sometimes see schools focusing on only the combative aspects of the art, missing the importance of the mental and spiritual components.

I just became the President of Modern Arnis International in the Philippines—an organization founded to preserve Professor Presas' art, and I also founded Arnis Maharlika—which is dedicated to promoting the Filipino Martial Arts. It would be wonderful to see Arnis as an event in the Olympics, and the overall goal is to preserve and promote FMA on a worldwide basis.

WORKING TOGETHER

If I could send a message to my brother and sister arnisadors all over the world it would be this: **unite**, **promote**, and **uplift** Modern Arnis worldwide. Let's support one another. We have a beautiful art and a wonderful founder. Consider the good things he gave us and share them with the world…

◊ BRUCE JUCHNIK ◊

I first met Remy in 1976. I had been studying martial arts for some time at that point, and when a friend asked me if I wanted to meet him, I said "yes," thinking that I would have an opportunity to 'school' him. When we met, he asked, "Bruce, you do the Filipino arts?" I said "yes" and proceeded to show him everything I knew. And when I was done, I asked him if he wanted to 'play.'

> **INVITATION TO PLAY**
>
> Those who knew the Professor remember that he would often approach a student and simply hold out his cane as an invitation to 'play.' Failure to respond would result in a directive to *'fractice'* whereas engaging would give rise to a flurry of techniques, the strength and tempo of which rapidly accelerated to the point of exhaustion.

In response to my challenge, Remy adjusted his glasses with his index finger and said, "Sure." He then proceeded to kick my ass, and I became his student then and there… After that, we traveled together a fair bit—in addition to being a warrior, Remy was a gypsy—and I got to participate in the introduction of Modern Arnis to venues across the country. I had the opportunity to get in on the ground floor.

> **THE POWER OF TOUCH**
>
> One of the most important things I learned from Remy was the power of touch. We used to spar with machetes, and when working with such dangerous weapons, it was important to be able to 'feel' the opponent's moves. On one particular occasion, I had decided to try to disarm him, but when I reached for the weapon, *it wasn't there*—he had switched hands!

ARNIS

Some people teach Modern Arnis as an add-on art, but I disagree with this: I believe that it should stand on its own as a complete art. I continued to study with Remy throughout his lifetime.

> ### THE IMPORTANCE OF POSTURE
>
> Another thing I learned with Remy was the importance of posture. If someone holds the *baston* too tightly, their legs will tighten, and they won't be able to defend against low strikes. Like Remy, I always try to adopt a lower, looser, stance so that I can defend high, low, and middle.

I currently teach several different art forms, one of which is Modern Arnis, and I teach it pretty much as it was taught to me by Remy. This is so because the art is more important than any one person. Another teacher of mine said that a true master lives 160 years, meaning that his art survives him. At the same time, one cannot learn from a teacher without absorbing some of his persona along the way. I am so grateful that I was able to absorb—and share—some of Remy's energy and art in my travels…

FILIPINO WARRIOR

♦ DIETER KNÜTTEL ♦

When I met Professor Remy Presas for the first time in 1994, I already had fifteen years of experience in Modern Arnis. I had trained a lot with his students Rodel Dagooc and Cristino Vasquez, as well as with his brothers Ernesto and Roberto and a lot of their students in the Philippines.

He was surprised to see twenty Modern Arnis black belts attending his seminar, wearing the uniform he had designed for Modern Arnis back in the 1960s in the Philippines—red pants, white T-shirt and the black belt rimmed with red—but you could see in his face that he liked what he saw. Anyway, the first meeting with Grandmaster Remy Presas was a special one. His Modern Arnis had gone through a lot of development compared to the Modern Arnis I had learned in the Philippines—more lock and takedown oriented, not so much striking, stabbing, and butting.

He was very smooth and soft with his movements. But this impression changed radically when you were his partner. When he had a grip on you, you felt like being trapped in a bench vise! There was no doubt that he would make his technique work, whatever you would do. That was very impressive and painful. It was beautiful to see though, how his combinations, locks, and takedowns interlinked with each other, and that this fitted in very well to what we had learned. Before, we concentrated on sinawali, striking counters, disarming techniques and other counters like that. We also had takedowns and locks, but his locks were more functional, direct, and effective.

It was nice to be able to enter a new world, with lots of things to learn, understand, and add to our program. After meeting the Professor, we changed our curriculum twice—once in 1996 and another time in 2002—to adapt the examination program to the new techniques and concepts we had learned from him. From the technical side, he was impressive: strong, powerful, and determined. I like to compare him with the "force of nature" that he was, even in his last years, when he was over sixty years of age.

Really amazing. But there was more to him, not only technically but also on a personal level, when leading and guiding to show us the right way. This impressed me more than any technique he ever demonstrated. He was so sure about himself and relaxed in who and what he was.

Always, when we had invited the Professor for a seminar, we also had black belt grading, so that he could see what we were teaching and what level our black belts held. Through watching the examinations, he knew our program and could have told us if we had not been on the right way. But he never did. Anyway, during one of the examinations we had a student going for Lakan Dalawa (second dan) who moved, to say it nicely, very individually. After the exam, when we sat together to discuss and decide who passed and who failed, we were not sure if this student was good enough, because his movements were rather unique. When we asked him about this student, Grandmaster Remy answered: "Give him his freedom." This taught us a lesson: How to deal with people who do not move like most of the others. Be tolerant and let them explore and express their way of doing things. On another occasion, two students were not good. In the discussion after the grading, he advised that we should give them provisionary black belts. This was again an example of how Grandmaster Remy always wanted to make people happy and did not want to hurt them.

In 1995, the Grandmaster started to teach Tapi-Tapi in Germany. Because we knew a very similar drill from his brother, freestyle sparring, we were curious to see how this would develop. Even though the drill was similar, there were a few very distinct differences. The most obvious one was that the "driver" of the drill applied the techniques with the stick in his *left* hand. He taught very systematically: First the twelve attacks with the counters, then the single Sinawali, then entering into the close distance for *punyo* and butt strikes, changing the stick to the left hand, starting with baiting and trapping techniques with both hands, and so on. The "drill" got bigger and bigger, and it was fascinating to see it grow and to understand how all the techniques linked with each other. To this day we keep the structure of his teaching when we introduce Tapi-Tapi to beginners.

TAPI-TAPI

The Buddha said: "Once upon a time there was a certain *raja* who called to his servant and said, 'Come, good fellow, go and gather together in one place all the men of Savatthi who were born blind... and show them an elephant.' 'Very good, sire,' replied the servant, and he did as he was told. He said to the blind men assembled there, 'Here is an elephant,' and to one man he presented the head of the elephant, to another its ears, to another a tusk, to another the trunk, the foot, back, tail, and tuft of the tail, saying to each one that that was the elephant. When the blind men had felt the elephant, the *raja* went to each of them and said to each, 'Well, blind man, have you seen the elephant? Tell me, what sort of thing is an elephant?' Thereupon the men who were presented with the head answered, 'Sire, an elephant is like a pot.' And the men who had observed the ear replied, 'An elephant is like a winnowing basket.' Those who had been presented with a tusk said it was a ploughshare. Those who knew only the trunk said it was a plough; others said the body was a grainery; the foot, a pillar; the back, a mortar; the tail, a pestle, the tuft of the tail, a brush..."

In his later years, the Professor began to emphasize the importance of Tapi-Tapi—counter-for-counter—in the practice of Modern Arnis. Depending on who is doing the teaching, drills illustrating this concept may emphasize entering from *sinawali*, striking with the *punyo*, fanning *abanico*-style, or trapping and locking. The truth is that each of these is an effective application of the core concept—a part of the elephant if you will.

Dieter Knüttel teaches Tapi-Tapi following a simple progression that he first learned from the Professor:*

1. Two partners ("the driver" and "the responder") begin by practicing exchanging strikes, blocks, and counters using the following rules:

A. The driver may attack using any angle, but when the responder attacks the driver's upper *left* region (using #1 or #3 strike), the driver does not "reply" in this same region. Similarly, if the responder attacks the

driver's upper *right* region (using #2 or #4), the driver does not reply in this same region.

B. The responder defends and "answers" the driver's strikes as quickly as possible, keeping his counters on the *same side* as the attack.

2. Once this pattern of exchanges is mastered, partners practice engaging in it from single *sinawali*.

3. They then introduce the idea of exchanging *punyo* strikes at *corto* range.

4. They then practice this method at all ranges (*corto=punyo* strikes; *medio*=strike/block; *largo=sinawali*) and switching among them.

5. The driver then practices switching from right to left hand and back in all three ranges, until a solid foundation is established.

6. The partners then introduce the techniques of stopping and grabbing the striking hand, and breaking free from such stops/grabs.

7. They then introduce entering with wing blocks and adding *abanico* strikes.

8. They then add in locking and trapping methods.

9. After all of this, any number of additional techniques and methods may be added…

This precept rests on the idea that for every action, there is a reaction, and for every reaction, there is a further response. As a result, when the practitioner's initial strike fails to find its mark, and in fact generates a responsive attack, that very response can be anticipated, manipulated, and exploited to good advantage. This teaching can be employed on a technical, tactical, and even strategic level. When performed perfectly, it is an absolutely devastating weapon, creating the impression that the practitioner has either seen the future or traveled in time.

* Video of this method being taught by Grandmaster/Datu Dieter Knüttel of the DAV (German Arnis Association) at various belt levels can be found here:

http://abanico.de/download/en/english_download_videos/modern-arnis-tapi-tapi-download-video

Here in Germany, in Europe, and with the help of the WBMA and other Modern Arnis groups worldwide, we will continue to work on the Grandmaster's dream of spreading Modern Arnis all over the world. His art will outlive us all, and one part of his dream has become true already: Modern Arnis is a well-respected and accepted martial art all over the world. Thank you, Professor Presas.

[Reprinted, with permission and many thanks, from 50 Years of Modern Arnis]

FILIPINO WARRIOR

ARNIS

♦ DOUG PIERRE ♦

Never forget that this is a war art! It is immediately deadly, period. That is why it is the main art I represent. I first started full-contact stick-fighting in 1989 at a tournament in New Jersey. For my first bout, they matched me up against a twenty-two year old, 250 pound champion (I was forty-five and 180 pounds at the time). I had no idea what I was doing. I had no strategy at all. He hit me so hard in the head that my helmet twisted around and I was looking out the ear hole! After that it was war! I went all out and after four two-minute rounds I was a puddle of sweat and my body would not relax for over an hour because of the adrenaline rush. Afterwards, people told me I didn't need to fight like that—I could have bobbed and weaved instead of going head on into the fray—and I wished I would have known that before. So after that I traveled around learning everything I could.

> ### ONE STRIKE TO RULE THEM ALL
>
> One of the big secrets in stick-fighting is that the Number Twelve strike can defeat every other strike. Just cutting down will block an attack from any other angle! I don't use anything too fancy—the basic angles, Abanico, Witik, Hirada, but I do them two ways: 'chopping' and 'cutting through.'

One of the special things about my relationship with Remy is that I didn't want anything from him (other than his knowledge). When Remy first found out I was going to fight in the Philippines, he tried to talk me out of it. He warned me that they would try to take advantage of me there. I think he was concerned that I would be putting his system on the line. When I got there, I had a lot of success, and many people approached me to see if I would represent their systems back in America. I said: "No, I'm

Remy's student and I'm loyal to him." I think they respected that. I have been back to the Philippines many times since then, and trained with many masters, in many systems, and I have always been welcome in everyone's school. In fact, I recently took one of my students there.

A WAR ART!

Not only did Doug test the Professor's system in the ring, in full-contact fighting; he did so in the Philippines, winning championships in 1992 (two gold medals) and 2016 (silver medal). In addition, Doug has gone on to train several students who have become champions in their own rights, including: Perry Zmugg, Patrick Paglen, Zarah Cabanas, and Phil Jones.

I am now seventy, and I'm thinking of competing at least one more time. I competed last year [at the age of sixty-nine] and the problem was that there was no one in my age group, so I had to fight guys in their thirties and forties!

One of the things that is most important to me going forward is to make sure that this art retains it deadliness. Another thing to keep in mind is that wherever we go, and whatever we do in this community, we all represent each other...

ARNIS

♦ JOHN RALSTON ♦

I attended my first "Big Three" seminar in Jacksonville, Florida, in October 1990. I will admit to being a bit nervous to meet and train with three martial arts legends. Headlining this amazing event were Professor Remy Amador Presas, Grandmaster George Dillman, and Professor Wally Jay. I had spent just over a year training in Ryukyu Kempo under the late Grandmaster Ed Lake at this time. This meant studying the VHS tapes of all three of the masters who would be teaching at the seminar that autumn weekend. By this point, Master Lake, had demonstrated to his students that there was a solid cohesion, if not a direct link, between all three of these martial arts systems. As Professor Presas would say, "You must make the connection!"

The students at the dojo I attended studied these tapes to the point where we believed we had a good understanding of the material. Remy's thick Filipino accent had become familiar and all of the students easily understood him. In fact, we would often good-naturedly mimic his accent at times in order to feel closer to him. Years later, many of those who were inspired by the Professor would continue to do this. Remy's encouraging words rang true to all: "This is lock. This is throw. This is takedown. This is lock also. BANG!" The intense study and power of the Professor, translated through his videos, served as a build up to meeting the masters.

After checking in, the other students who travelled to the seminar and I quickly dropped our luggage in the hotel rooms. As a group, we headed out the pool area, hoping to catch a glimpse of the masters at rest. Walking past the pool, we spotted a few people in a hot tub. Ed Lake excitedly rushed up, his students following behind. There in the hot tub were two of the grandmasters: George Dillman and Remy Presas. Ed exchanged pleasantries with them, and discussed where *karaoke* was going to be held later that night. Master Lake made introductions and I could not seem muster much more than a single, "Hello."

I was both awed and stunned at the same time. I thought that the grandmasters would be in uniform, training, not relaxing and laughing as good friends. My wife, who joined me on the trip as a fellow student, said that my smile lasted the rest of the night following meeting some of my heroes. During the first session of training, the Professor was every bit the charismatic, dynamic ball of passionate energy I had found him to be on video. He worked his way around the room, helping attendees with the technique he had just shown. When he approached my training partner and me, he asked us what style we studied. "Ryukyu Kempo," we replied. With a booming voice, the Professor announced, "Then you are my brothers!" He hugged us tightly then. Professor Presas was as warm and generous as I had imagined him to be. I found myself somewhat star-struck and dumbfounded yet again. Maybe I had been hit in the head with a stick... Likely not, though, as so many others had similar experiences when meeting the Professor for the first time.

The next time I had the opportunity to train with the Professor, he pulled me by the arm towards a group that was being instructed by one of his senior students. He then said loudly to me, "John this is Bram. He will be your teacher when you cannot see me." To the man teaching the group, he stated simply, "Bram this is John. You will show him the way!" Many years later, Datu Bram Frank, and I still joke about how we met. Bram often tells people that Remy 'gave me' to him. I tell him, "I'm the one student he can never get rid of because Remy said so!"

I was extremely privileged to train with the Professor throughout the 1990s, in no small part due to his fondness for south Florida. The beaches and weather, he often said, reminded him of his home in the Philippines. Being his *uke* brought with it a special kind of pain, but also a great opportunity to understanding what he was teaching. During much of this time, I was working the overnight shift as an auditor at a five-star resort and hotel in Fort Lauderdale. The Professor would often call me to arrange to stay at the hotel. His calls to me were short and simple: "John, I am coming to see you. Can you put me in the hotel?"

This was utterly fantastic for me because while he was at the hotel, Bram and I, and a few others would get some personal training. On one occasion, the Professor came to stay during Thanksgiving. My family and I had the great honor of having him as a holiday guest. Of course, he carved the turkey! Training with Professor Presas, along with Grandmaster Dillman and Professor Wally Jay, was an incredibly special time for me, not only in terms of growth in skill as a martial artist, but in relation to personal growth as well. The Professor's passing was far too early, and it taught me an additional lesson: Never put off training with the masters, doing what you love, or spending time with those you love. Too often, you will find yourself thinking: "I wish I had gone to that event or spent more time with them..."

◊ **MICHELLE RALSTON** ◊

Like many others, I first met the larger-than-life Professor Remy Amador Presas at the now-famous "Big Three" martial arts seminars in Jacksonville, Florida. I was very young when I first met the Professor and he immediately recognized my nervousness, but also my eagerness to learn. He told me that I was to call him "Papa Remy" as he was now also my father. On one of Papa Remy's many visits to Miami Beach, my then-boyfriend and I were on the sand, ready to train before the sun was up. My now-husband and Datu Bram Frank were busily flowing from one drill to another while Papa Remy called out a seemingly unending list of different techniques. I took my turn with the two of them, trying to keep up as best I could.

At some point, Papa called me over to sit with him at a shaded table where he was watching the men training. He then produced a *Balisong* knife from what seemed like thin air, and proceeded to show me some of the applications of this unique blade, guiding me through a number of drills. On more occasions than I could possibly remember, he would quietly teach me what he thought was "especial for a young lady to learn."

During these sunny beachside training sessions, I would look after my Filipino father and he would make sure that "Michelina" (his special name for me) would learn everything the men were being taught. On one especially hot day, I noticed two gallon-sized bottles of water that he had placed on the nearby table. I asked if he was thirsty. He laughed a bit and said, "No, Michelina. Those are for work out!" I learned that it was a common practice for him to travel with empty gallon bottles in his luggage, and then fill them with water at his destination in order to use them for weights while working out.

During one training session on the sand, a group of young men noticed the sounds of the banging sticks and quickly came over to watch. The Professor pocketed the knife he was using to demonstrate a certain technique for me and greeted the new group, asking where they were from. He acted as a cultural ambassador for the Philippines in his newly adopted country. He shared the beauty of the art with this group rather than demonstrating some of the more deadly applications of the blade. After they had moved on, he gave my now-husband a serious looked and said: "John, you must make certain my Michelina knows this. You will show her the way." My husband stammered, "But sir, I didn't see what you did!" At this, he let loose with his infectious belly laugh: "Ha, ha, ha! I am the grandmaster. Do as I say!"

Many long years have passed since those first days training with Papa Remy. Nevertheless, I still hear his voice and feel his spirit in his many students from around the world—even from students who had never had the opportunity to meet this amazing teacher of the art. I miss Papa Remy every day…

FILIPINO WARRIOR

Arnis

♦ Larry Rocha ♦

Remy wasn't just a great teacher; he was a great person—his charisma just filled the room.

I remember the first time I met him at a seminar in the mid-80s. I had no idea what he was doing, but I was hooked right away and decided, "I've got to stay with this." At the end of the seminar there was a test. I hadn't planned on testing because I was so new to the art, but one of the candidates needed a partner, so I volunteered to help. After the test was over, the Professor came up to me and said, "You are Larry, right? Do not test again!" I thought to myself, "Jeez, I didn't think I was *that* bad!" But then he explained further, "You are my student, you will test with me." I guess he must have liked some of what I did! When he promoted me to Lakan, he came to stay with me for a few days. We trained intensely for two straight days—ten to twelve hours a day—at the end of which he gave me a few whacks on butt and said: "You are now Lakan." Then we went to get something to eat!

Bite-sized Chunks

The Professor was so impressive when he was demonstrating techniques. Many people had trouble following everything he was doing. One thing I learned early on that the best way to learn from the Professor—for me anyway—was just to focus on picking up the first one or two things, and then come back later once I had absorbed those things to learn more.

Over the years that followed, I trained with the Professor at many seminars, both in my area and elsewhere. In fact, he used to love to come and stay with us at the beach—he said it reminded him of the Philippines.

He truly became part of our family.

I remember on one occasion we were at a restaurant in the Boston area. The Professor started the meal by ordering a salad with 'Filipino dressing.' The waitress told him they did not have Filipino dressing, but he replied, "Yes you do—thousand island!" At some point, he had to walk through the bar to get to the bathroom. Along the way, he must have bumped into one of the customers, because this big guy suddenly stood up and said to him, "Watch were you are going you stupid Eskimo!" Remy said, "I am sorry, but I am not an Eskimo, I am Filipino." The other guy wouldn't leave it alone and kept pushing him, so finally the Professor locked him up (without hurting him too much) and said, "I told you: I am not an Eskimo, I am Filipino! Now, I must go to the bathroom…" Then he let him go, went to the bathroom, came back to our table, sat down, and started eating like nothing had happened! That's the kind of guy he was …

◊ BRETT SALAFIA ◊

Professor Remy Presas was a master and innovator in the Filipino martial arts. His speed, timing, power, and innovation were second to none. Most of his students continue to refine the lessons he shared with them about his life's work: Modern Arnis. But lessons learned on the mat—sometimes with a new bruise or injury—are only part of the story. Many students missed the bigger picture of the Professor's lessons. While his stick, knife, and empty hand teachings are the reason that most people trained with him, the evolution of his system over time serves as a guidebook to personal growth in any aspect of life. The Professor's observation regarding the personal growth of his students validated his life's work.

Arnis

The Professor and I spent a good deal of time together during my three years of law school. We trained in Modern Arnis regularly in the southern United States. He understood acutely some of the sacrifices that were necessary in order to continue training in Modern Arnis and studying the law simultaneously. His sense of pride was obvious when I received my degree. It was not the nature of that achievement, but rather the personal growth that really impressed him. Today, more than sixteen years after his death, I continue to reflect on the influence this one man had on my life.

The Professor helped me achieve a variety of life goals. It is cliché at best, but when confronted with difficult situations I still consider how he would approach them. Several aspects of his teachings come into play when I try to channel his spirit in order to confront challenges. Three common "Professor-isms" serve to provide guidance for me both on and off the mat:

Practice: The first is practice. It would be difficult to quantify the number of times the Professor reminded students that they must practice something. It sounded like: "You must *practice*. Make it slow…" Too often students did not follow this important advice. The Professor was a study in practice. He learned, refined, practiced, and re-refined his skills regularly. He trained with many different people to learn the limits of human movement. This high level analysis framed his daily practice. If you were lucky enough to spend time with him off the mat, you know that he was always practicing. Even while sailing down the Mississippi River on a warm fall afternoon, he trained his art. Of course the tedious nature of practice frustrates many students. But regular practice is the *only* way to develop a skill. The Professor spoke about learning secrets from Balintiwak founder Anciong Bacon; *after* plying him with ham and American liquor. Even when the Professor was armed with the three secrets of Arnis, it was *practice* that made them useful.

Connections: Next comes the concept of connections. The Professor constantly encouraged students to make connections. In the martial context, this meant beginning to see the relationship between concepts. This allows the savvy student to take material and expand on it for different situations. A simple example might be the mirror image relationship between the *abanico corto* and *palis-palis* applications from a forehand strike. Understanding the power of connection multiplies these techniques exponentially. But merely identifying connections is not enough. The application of connections to a given situation requires the ability to identify, categorize, and prioritize each individual connection to maximize its effect. Of course, seeking out connections and making them relevant also requires practice. The real lesson was that connections between people and ideas multiply our understanding of the world around us. It could be as simple as networking. Through the Professor, I have a network that covers many cities, states, and countries. With a call or an e-mail, I can find a place to stay, or a person with whom to share a meal. These human connections cross all manner of races, genders, politics, vocations and ages. Our basic connection is the Professor's art, but in the form of a passion for personal growth. Artists, fighters, thinkers, and do-ers all relate to this basic connection through the Professor. And acknowledging and embracing these unique qualities in people, places, things or concepts lead us to the last concept:

It Is All The Same: The concept that "it is all the same" is maddening to a neophyte in the martial arts. It is difficult to fathom sameness while struggling to retain new information. There is a day when practice of basics and searching for martial connections finally illuminates this concept, much like a lightbulb turning on. The lines of individual movement and particular techniques are suddenly erased. Instead, the ability to tackle problems begins to flow without regard for pre-defined starting or ending points. This sameness and flow are the essence of Modern Arnis. The system is stripped away and movement begins and ends seamlessly.

Professor Remy Presas gave his students a blueprint for life:

• Practice no matter how well you think you know something. Keep practicing and keep refining.

• Understand the connections that make up your world. How do these connections affect any given goal.

• And exploit the sameness that is around you.

Through careful practice and understanding of connections you will ultimately see that Professor was right: "It really *is* all the same…"

ARNIS

◊ KEN SMITH ◊

I first met the Professor at a seminar in Joliet Illinois in 1992, and right away I knew I was going to follow him for the rest of my life. There were over a hundred people there, but after the seminar I went right up to Remy and told him this was the most impressive thing I'd ever seen, and that I wanted to learn everything he had to teach. He said, "OK, where you live?" I told him I was local. He said, "Oh, you must go to George Mazek." So George became my first Modern Arnis instructor, and the best thing about it was that he was also an instructor under [then] Master George Dillman, so I got Ryukyu Kempo at the same time, and didn't even know at first that they weren't the same thing!

I trained with George Mazek up to Lakan Isa (First Degree Black Belt), and then the Professor took a more direct interest in me because I was going to every seminar I could, traveling wherever I could go to train with him. At one point he told me to meet him at a particular seminar to be his uke. Now being someone's uke has its plusses and minuses, but I think anytime you can get the Grandmaster's hands on you, it's a pretty good idea, because then you know exactly how the technique is supposed to feel. So I was happy to do it, but I felt like I should ask for George's permission first, but Professor Presas got mad at me! He said, "You do not have to ask permission! I am the Grandmaster!" I explained that I meant no disrespect to him, but wanted to show proper respect to Mr. Mazek as well. And he said, "From now on, you are my student, directly to me!" And that's how it happened…

Everyone who trained with, or even met, Professor Presas knew that he was one of the kindest souls imaginable. But it has to be kept in mind that he learned his art in a different time and place. He came up the hard way, fighting in contact tournaments in the Philippines, and this climate differed from that of the United States on a number of different levels. He sometimes found American customs and practices unusual, and the same was true in reverse from time-to-time.

For many years Chuck Gauss, Jim Ladis and I travelled everywhere we could with the Professor. These were some pretty talented guys. Jim [Ladis] is legally blind—has been since he began training with the Grandmaster—but to see his technique, you'd never guess. To this day I love to watch Chuck Gauss work, and when I watch him, I always pick up things. The same is true with Dr. Randi Schea. Chuck is a big guy and the Professor trained him differently than he trained me. He learned big, powerful technique. I am smaller—almost exactly the same size as the Professor—so I learned to move quickly, like the Professor. And Dr. Schea was trained differently from either one of us because he's 135 pounds and 5'3". So now, we all have different things we can share with each other.

The Professor's system has eight open hand forms and four stick forms (five if you count the variation: Anyo Dalawa, Four Corners). Not a lot of people know that the Professor had a background in Shotokan Karate. He trained with Funakoshi's number two student and earned the rank of Sixth Degree Black Belt. So if you look at some of the Anyos (Forms), especially the higher level ones, you'll see that they are like Filipino Shotokan! And since a lot of his forms were based on Shotokan, they contain some of the ancient pressure point principles from before his time. In the Philippines, every technique can be turned into a drill. A drill is just a way to teach a technique. Most people end up looking toward the Filipino arts because of that. As the Professor would say, "Repetition is the mother of learning. You must repeat." And how do you repeat without making it boring? You put it in a continuous drill. "No stop. This is the best." So Abanico or Banda-y-Banda can easily be made into a drill in the same way that Sinawali or Redonda have been.

What the Professor taught changed over time. I think that in the beginning this was, at least in part, because when he was fighting in the Philippines, he didn't want to give away his best techniques in case somebody might have been faster than him and used his own tricks against him. Beyond that, though, he was always working on what he called, "the innovations," and he encouraged his students to do the same, to, "make it yours." One of my proudest moments was coming up with a technique while working with one of my students and when I showed it to him, his response was, "Oh, we will teach this to everyone." And he did. So in some small way, I feel like I was able to give him something back. Even for me, I move the way he taught me to move, but I have added in certain things, like pressure points, to what I do.

For example, with left-handed combination: Sweep-stroke-enter-parry-backfist-parry-hold (the first left-handed technique he taught to almost everybody), I still do it the way he did it, exactly as he taught me. The only difference is that I aim for certain pressure points in the process—Lung 6, Stomach 5, and I hold for the knockout.

Modern Arnis can be a very deadly art. People will sometimes try to downplay its effectiveness. But when you talk about combat-effectiveness, it depends what your definition of "combat" is. For example, most people agree that mixed martial arts ("MMA") fighters are some of the toughest guys around—I have nothing but respect for what they do—but nevertheless, there are certain rules in the ring: No small joint manipulation; no eye gouging; no hitting when a man's down. Now that still makes for a tough fight, but it's a little different from a fight to the death. If you're fighting for your life on the street, you're going to want a weapon in your hand, and who's going to do it better? A Filipino stick or knife guy. Now I would never want to use the Professor's art to hurt somebody—he taught us always to use it for good—but sometimes good is surviving. Master Gauss was a police officer for many years and used the art to protect himself and others. I work part-time as a process-server and can think of at least three occasions where I've had to use it to defend myself. So it depends on what you think "combat" is.

VENANCIO "ANCIONG" BACON

♦ DR. CHARLES TERRY ♦

I began training in Modern Arnis in 1988. At that time, Michael Bates and I were training together in Ryukyu Kempo. Michael had just gone to a "Triple Seminar" featuring Wally Jay, George Dillman, and Remy Presas at Jim Clapp's school in Delaware. He was very excited about Modern Arnis and shared what he had learned with me.

Soon thereafter, I met Professor Presas at another seminar. It was easy to see why Modern Arnis was destined to become a major part of our training. Professor Presas was simply amazing! He would teach a basic technique, and then ten variations and follow-throughs on this move. I can still hear him say, *"I'd like to see you do that!"* All of the students would look at each other and try to figure out what the original technique was! Fortunately, the Professor would come around the room and give personal attention to everyone until we got it. *"Make it slow,"* he would say.

MAKE IT SLOW...

I often relate martial arts practice to learning a musical instrument. The way to learn any difficult passage is to start slowly. When it starts to click, it's easy to pick up the tempo. I have also found this pearl of wisdom to apply to life in general when things get too overwhelming—slow things down by focusing on just **one** thing.

When I started college in 1986, I founded the University of Pennsylvania Ryukyu Kempo Club. We quickly began incorporating Modern Arnis into the curriculum, and I encouraged my students to attend as many seminars as they could. Professor Presas made such an impact on me, and had so many connections throughout the martial arts world, that had I not gotten into medical school, I planned to spend the year after college travelling and training with him. As fate would have it, however, I was admitted to medical school and had to settle for Arnis summer camps and seminars that weren't too far away. I continued to train and teach.

By the end of medical school, I was able to save up some vacation time before starting residency. I will always treasure the two months in 1994 when I got to travel up and down the East Coast (and to Texas) with Professor Presas. It was not uncommon for him to say, *"Pull over here"* when we were driving if inspiration mandated immediate practicing! He was even kind enough to help with my traveling expenses. That same year I began sponsoring triple seminars (Jay-Dillman-Presas) in the Philadelphia area.

> ### THE SHIRT OFF HIS BACK
>
> At one point I asked the Professor where I could get one of those cool Arnis uniforms. Without hesitation, he took off the Arnis top he was wearing and gave it to me! He was so generous, he literally gave me the shirt off his back (yes, I have washed it since then!). In July 1991, I earned my black belt in Modern Arnis at the Mount Holy Oak Camp.

My main student base at that time was young, healthy, college students. During an Arnis Camp, I told the Professor about our black belt tests: About eight hours long, comprehensive, including aspects of all four styles, and <u>no breaks</u>. He said, *"Don't you want to be a doctor? Your students must drink water to be healthy!"* From that day on, water breaks (and even lunch breaks) were included in our black belt tests—and I tell the candidates that they can all thank Professor Presas for the breaks!

During our travels, the Professor took me to an importer of rattan and taught me how to make Arnis sticks:

⊗ First, choose straight rattan—three-quarters of an inch to an inch-and-a-quarter in diameter—with the skin on (to increase durability).

⊗ Then, cut into appropriate lengths (usually 26-28 inches). Sticks can then be paired with similar coloring, grain, diameters, and nodes.

⊗ The most important part is sanding the ends for safety so there are no sharp edges.

⊗ He also taught me how to burn patterns on the sticks and add lacquer, if desired, for a more 'polished' look. I dabbled briefly in the production and sale of Arnis sticks, but the rigors of medical school soon put an end to that endeavor.

I will forever be thankful for the quality time the Professor spent with me sharing this aspect of his beloved art.

> ### FIRST DO NO HARM!
>
> We were at a seminar in Maryland when two different students got clipped over the eyebrow and it broke the skin. One needed stitches; the other refused to leave the seminar so we used a butterfly bandage. We inspected the sticks they were using, and it was clear that the ends had not been sanded. The simple precaution of telling everyone to rub the ends of their stick against a cinder block or cement significantly reduced the risk of further injury...

Often when Professor Presas was in town, we would visit Asian World of Martial Arts. They invited him to a photo shoot for their new catalogue. He was excited to do anything that would help to spread his beloved art. He instantly saw this as an opportunity to advertise Modern Arnis. For the better part of a day, I got a private lesson with him as his partner during the photography. He was on the next year's catalogue cover. They did not, however, use any pictures of me—apparently, my 'pained expression' (however legitimate) appeared too staged! I was paid one dollar for my trouble, but every time I see the Professor's picture in the weapons' section of their current catalogues I think of the time I was honored to be involved with that photo shoot.

In 1997, I opened MKA Karate and officially coined the term: "Modern Kempo Association." This is a combination of Modern Arnis, Small-Circle Jujitsu, Wei Kuen Do, and Ryukyu Kempo (our students train in all four styles). Rather than creating a new system with **elements** of each style, the Modern Kempo Association allows students to earn rank in **each individual system** and make their own connections, as the original Grandmasters and first generation students have done. Over the years, we have sponsored seminars with each of the Grandmasters (with Leon Jay taking over for his father when Wally Jay's health no longer permitted travel). We continue to welcome Grandmasters from each of the arts.

> ### THE LAST ACT
>
> A few words should be said about the Professor's final seminar. It took place in Philadelphia in 2001. Already terminally ill at this time, the Professor 'escaped' from his hospital room in Canada to be with his friends and colleagues one last time, arriving at the seminar with nothing but the

> clothes on his back! We soon realized that he did not even have the medication he was supposed to be taking with him! Fortunately, I was able to consult with another doctor in the organization and write prescriptions which Michael Bates then kindly filled. I gave the Professor one final acupuncture treatment at Michael's house and, when he developed pneumonia, helped get him admitted to Riddle Memorial Hospital. Michael—who should be commended for his service in this regard—took it from there, eventually helping the Professor return to Canada for the last time...

With the Professor's passing, there is no longer one clear head-of-system for Modern Arnis (as there is for the other three systems). Rather than choosing to join just one branch exclusively, MKA has remained open to all. We are grateful to Michael Bates for creating the Hall of Fame Foundation—an association of equals that is open to everyone—and a place where masters from every branch of the Modern Arnis family tree can come together to share students, techniques, and ideas, and to honor the Founder.

In an effort to ensure that our students continue to live up to widely-accepted standards within the Modern Arnis community, MKA is in the process of developing a curriculum, set forth in rough form below, which is largely based on the Professor's original video series. In keeping with the Remy Presas approach to art and life, this is an organic process, and we are open to suggestions from any interested practitioners...

FILIPINO WARRIORS

COME TOGETHER

As a practitioner who came to the art fairly early on, trained extensively with the Professor in the years that followed, and remained his direct student until the very end, Dr. Terry is one of a handful of senior Modern Arnis practitioners named by Remy Presas in his will(s) to serve as a member of a board intended to promote, teach, and preserve the art after his passing. His students regularly attend the annual Hall of Fame summer camp in Villanova, Pennsylvania, and he has developed strong working relationships with a broad array of senior masters in this art.

Under Dr. Terry's leadership, MKA Karate is in the process of developing a Modern Arnis syllabus that is intended to codify the fundamental techniques and forms shared by many—if not most—of the branches of the Modern Arnis family tree—a kind of common core curriculum. Suggestions and comments in this regard will be welcomed (via: remypresasstories@gmail.com), as the ultimate goal is to promote unity within the Modern Arnis community.

RANK	FORM	MINIMUM REQUIREMENTS
Orange (Antas Dalawa)	----	• Twelve Angles, Block-Check-Counter, Single Sinawali
Yellow (Antas Tatlo)	Stick 1 (Anyo Isa)	• Redonda, Disarms 1-6
Green (Antas Apat)	Open 1 (Anyo Isa)	• Double Sinawali, Disarms 7-12
Blue (Antas Lima)	Stick 2 (Anyo Dalawa)	• Reverse Sinawali, Six Count Drill
Purple (Antas Anim)	Open 2 (Anyo Dalawa)	• Single Sinawali Applications, Trap Hands
Brown (Likha)	Stick 3 (Anyo Tatlo)	• Double Sinawali Apps, Sinawali Box Drill Block/Check/Counter/Counter
Brown 1 (Likha Isa)	Open 3 (Anyo Tatlo)	• Rev. Sinawali Apps, Disarm Counters 1-6
Brown 2 (Likha Dalawa)	Stick 4 (Anyo Apat)	• Abanico (corto y largo) with Apps, Disarm Counters 7-12, Stick Spar (basic)
Brown 3 (Likha Tatlo)	Open 4 (Anyo Apat)	• Stick sparring (advanced), Knife Self-defense
Prob. Black (Lakan/Dayang)	Open 5 (Anyo Lima)	• Tapi-Tapi, Baiting with Traps and Throws; Espada y daga
Black Belt (Lakan/Dayang Isa)	Open 6 (Anyo Anim)	• Moving With the Flow • Advanced Apps Drills and Forms • Minimum 16 YOA/1 Year at Lakan

ARNIS

♦ DENNIS TOSTEN ♦

I first learned about Remy from two of my students who attended a camp—maybe the first one—in North Carolina in the 1980s. They came back and told me, "This guy is great!" I then met him myself at a seminar in Philadelphia and we hit it off right away!

A PHILOSOPHY OF KINDNESS

You only go around this thing once, and you want to be the right person on that trip. You want to keep the negativity out of your mind, your talk, and your life. Remy was like that...

The ceiling of the room was covered in smoke from all the stick-on-stick contact. It was like a fog! I loved his stuff right away. It was so different from what I had been doing up to that point. And it made what I was doing so much better—my defenses, my knife work. It really was the art within my art.

THE CHICKEN HAND

One of my favorite memories of Remy's teachings was what we called 'the chicken hand.' During the early days, he would sometimes say to us: "Chicken, CHICKEN!" One day I asked him what he meant by that, and he explained: "*Chick han*—check the hand!"

After that he used to say to me: "You know, when you started with me, you were a duck—quack quack! Now you are a tiger: 'Tiger Tosten!'"

◊ KELLY WORDEN ◊

I was one of Cui Brocka's students, like Datu Dieter Knuttel. Cui was teaching at Fort Lewis. I did the research and found out that he was training under Ernesto Presas, and when I saw that the big brother (Remy Presas) was in town, I went and saw him. Wow! There was so much difference. It was such a balanced art.

At that time it wasn't convenient for me to train with him, and I had notions of being loyal, so it was another year before I had the opportunity to go and meet the Professor. That was courtesy of Leonard Trigg—he organized the first seminar in the northwest at the Oregon Athletic Center.

After training with the Professor for many years, I asked him, "Why did you beat me like a red-headed step-child?"

He said, "Well, you are quite tough, and if I can make you cry like a little baby boy, then everyone will pay attention!"

THE KNIFE

The Professor was intrigued by the fact that I was teaching combat controllers and servicemen at the naval base in Tacoma. This is why he told me to specialize in the knife. He said, "I don't want to be known as a master of everything, a jack of all trades. I have the *bolo* but I don't want to scare people." He wanted to spread the art. He was the guy who could empower anybody.

It was really his teaching methodology that I embraced. To me it was a path to Jeet Kune Do, a path to FMA that was freely expressed, and I understood why he did the different things he did, and why he had a renegade attitude. We meshed well.

> ### THE STAFF
>
> The Professor really liked the staff *(sibat)*. When I showed him my techniques, he correlated them with the Modern Arnis Anyos and showed me how it all translated. He could connect any dot, so if he was leading you down a path and you didn't take the bait, well that was *your* problem! People say the weapon is just an extension of the hand but, very few people can actually prove that. Professor Presas was one of them. Wally Jay said, 'I can show him *anything* and he adapts to it.'

Mastery of a technique doesn't mean simply performing the beats of that movement, but entails understanding the underlying reasons and the minor actions between the beats. Your chamber move is a deployment. You are executing movements. Every time you retract, that is a point of acquisition and deployment of your tools and your weapons. There is *so much* to simplicity. Simplicity is the connection to versatility.

> ### KATA
>
> Kata is everything; that is the structural integrity of freedom. If you don't know how to stabilize your base, you are just a free-standing swing guy. Where is the science? The science is in the structural integrity of the old ways. What is taken out is the aliveness. I came with the aliveness; now give me structure and oh my god, you have put the tools together for me! Anyo is such a beautiful thing, even if it is just a figure eight.

To me, the most important aspect of the art is the Flow. The Flow brings me into the moment of aliveness. People sometimes say, "It looks like Worden is making it up as he goes along," but what is a fight? If you can't improvise, you have already lost. If you are bound by technique, you are involved in a sport. Life is not a sport, reality is not a sport. The fight isn't **on** until you touch. It is vital that a fighter can close and hit, that he can isolate and neutralize the threat—*that* is what the Professor brought to the table.

In the FMA it is important to be able to read structure and posture. Without this, you can't analyze movement; you can't isolate and align yourself; you can't gain positional control. Kata teaches you positional control. *Naihanchi* is a classic example of foot trapping, of attachment, of positional alignment, of structural manipulation, of the ability to close or touch or move on the opponent. Once you become engaged, that is attainment, and you never disengage. People need to understand the longevity of the engagement. When you move, you move the opponent with you. Once I start, I stay with the opponent at every step. Everything is an attack by drawing, using him as a body shield, everything is based on those elements. Form without intent is just pretty stuff.

> ### THE PRESAS LEGACY
>
> I designed and created a blade with the Professor. He suggests making it *doublete* and I really like that because there is a back edge. He looked at in silhouette and said, 'It is the goddess of the knife!' I said, "The steel will outlive us all," and he really liked that. We ultimately called it "The Presas Legacy." He was really tickled about that. It was a beautiful moment...

I connect all arts to Modern Arnis; it doesn't matter what it is I teach, the roots go there. You have to research and understand how it all links. I connect Jesse Glover art with Sonny Umpad's, Richard Bustilio's, Ted Lucylucay's, Wally Jay's; and it is *all* Modern Arnis. My art is not traditional. "Modern" means that it is always growing...

FILIPINO WARRIORS

ARNIS

◊ Don Zanghi ◊

I first met Remy in 1983 at a Camp in the hills of West Virginia that was owned by Priscilla Presley. I had broken a bone in my hand and was in a cast at the time, but the people running the Camp told me that it wouldn't be a problem. After a week of training there, I was having trouble holding onto the cane and actually lost my grip on it at one point! I couldn't stay for the second week of training and testing—I had a job to get back to in New York—and was told that I would not be awarded a provisional rank. I was disappointed, but as I was walking toward my cabin to pack and depart, the Professor just appeared on the path behind me and told me to accompany him to his room where he promoted me to brown belt (provisional) on the spot! I was so new to all of this that I actually asked him if he would get in trouble for doing so…

Not long after this Camp, Remy called me and told me that he would be in New York and asked me to help him set up some teaching events. In typical Remy fashion, there was not a lot of lead-time! As luck would have it, there was a film crew at the airport chasing another story when I went to pick him up, and I tipped them off to the fact that a martial arts grandmaster would be arriving shortly. Fortunately they were quite interested, and ran a short piece about the Professor on the news that evening. This was the same weekend that Bill Adams—a local legend—was holding his annual CAN-AM tournament, and I didn't want to be disrespectful by appearing to compete with him, so I contacted him and explained the situation. Again, luck was with us as he invited us to come and do an exhibition at his event. In fact, when we got there, Remy gave me just a few minutes to teach the basics of Arnis to Bill's top student, but when the demonstration was all over, everyone understood the power of the system. To my knowledge, this was the first time Modern Arnis was brought to Western New York, and the art is still thriving there today.

I should add that this was also Thanksgiving week, and we had invited the Professor to join us for our family get-together. It was here that he first learned about American football. We tried to keep his presence secret, but word got out, and so many of my neighbors came to see the Grandmaster that we ended up moving all of the furniture in my Aunt's living room to make space for him to give a demonstration of his art in action!

> ## STEALTH
>
> One of the things I learned from Remy was the importance of stealth, both on and off the mat. The first time I met him—and on many occasions after that—he would simply appear, to everyone's surprise, in one location or another, having quietly arrived, or moved from one position to the next, unnoticed. This is a great tool in combat as well as in life.

I went on to blend Modern Arnis with the Kenpo I was already teaching. Remy explained to me once that there was a strong linkage between these two arts as they had blended and matured—along with many others—in the Hawaiian Islands because of their proximity to the birthplace of so many different martial arts.

Even after retiring from running a school and moving to Florida in the 1990s, I kept in touch with the Professor and a handful of students. Once he came to visit me there and I had the opportunity to introduce him to some of my own students as well as a local martial arts instructor. And even though we did not train much on this final visit—he was in poor health at the time—it was a chance to share his remarkable personality with a few people who had never had the opportunity to meet him before.

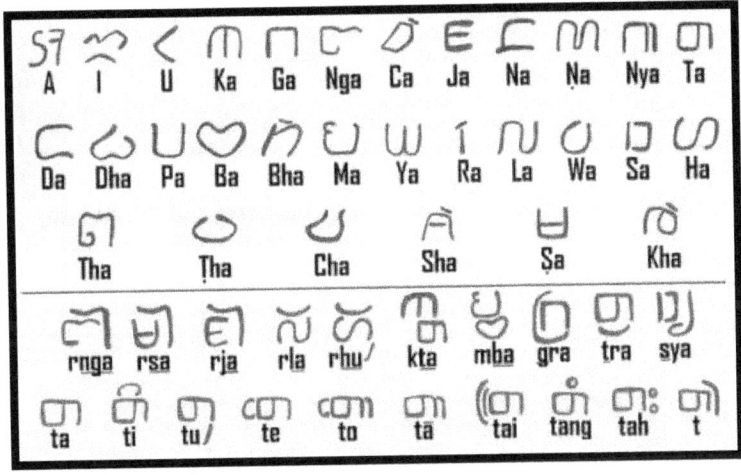

Arnis

♦ Brian Zawilinski ♦

I started training with Professor Lee Lowery in Tracy Kenpo in July of 1981.[1] Shortly after I started training with him, he went to a seminar with what he was told was, "some guy teaching sticks." Of course Kenpo has a long history of crossing over with the Filipino arts, so it seemed logical. When Professor Lowery came back he was very excited and motivated. He said, "Oh, you will meet him…" In the summer of 1982, Professor Lowery had Professor Presas come in to teach the first of many seminars. I was fourteen years old at the time, but I still remember having Professor Presas sign two books for me. I still have those books to this day.

Left Lead

On one occasion, Professor Presas wanted to do a demonstration with Professor Lowery using live machetes! Professor Lowery kept trying to talk him out of it, saying he didn't have the skills (at that time) to keep up, but as we all know, when Professor Presas wanted do something, he did it. Professor Presas said, "Do not worry, it is OK!" When they came up to demonstrate, the room was silent; you could have heard a pin drop. If you have experienced the sound that machetes make when they clash, it stays with you. Once you have heard it, you do not forget it! They started with single siniwalli and then shifted into rolling/butting (the original solo baston semi-sparring). At some point, Professor Presas really turned it on, and ended up shifting to a left-hand lead (he was a natural southpaw). It ended up with Professor Lowery being disarmed, his right arm pinned against his side, and Professor Presas' machete pinned in his armpit, edge up, against his body!

Many years later when Professor Presas began teaching the left-on-right tapi-tapi, I thought about that early demonstration of the left-lead and I

---

[1] As used here, the title "Professor" refers to Lowery's ultimate Kenpo rank and should not be confused with Arnis ranking.

> asked him, "Why release the left side now?" He laughed, and said, "I was bored!" He then explained that he hadn't practiced that way over the years, but, "Once you have it you do not forget it." The concept stays with you…

In the years following that first seminar, Professor Presas would come to Connecticut frequently, often staying with Professor Lowery for a week at a time to train. At the same time, I started working for the state, ultimately beginning a career in Corrections, which has been a blessing for me to this day. At the same time, I have been able to work with a lot of high caliber students and veteran instructors in the martial arts.

LEARN BY WATCHING

> Professor Presas could just watch something and then own it; he was always watching and always learning. I remember how he would end camps by saying, "Thank you" to the students because he always learned from watching them.

I have been fortunate in that I don't depend on the martial arts for my livelihood (I know it is not an easy path). For folks like myself, Chad Dulin, and Larry Rocha, this has meant that we can pursue our martial goals on our own terms. Obviously, as a student of the martial arts, working in corrections has served as part of my education. I won't claim to have seen everything, but I have certainly seen a lot! I think that not having to rely on the arts to make a living has allowed me to "pay it forward" and be more flexible with my time in good faith in an effort to further the arts.

IT IS ALL THE SAME

> I don't have a favorite technique or group of techniques; I try to embrace Professor's saying that, "It is all the same." When I was younger, I took that to mean that the techniques of Modern Arnis were all that same—you have *banda y banda* or *rompida* striking styles, but all of these classical striking styles are just variations on a theme with changes in angle and direction—but after the Professor's death, and decades of this concept saturating my brain, it became clear that he meant all martial arts were ultimately the same; that movement was movement. One of my students has been studying Tai Chi for well over a decade. Early on in his studies, I went to watch a session. Later I commented to him, "That Tai Chi master is a hell of an arnis player!" The art doesn't matter. It does not matter what you have in your hand. It is all relative and the connection is always there…

ARNIS

The discord and controversy within the Arnis world following Professor Presas' death was unfortunate, but as things have shaken out, the art has begun spreading again. People are more willing to train together across organizations—they train together without issues and across stylistic lines. People are researching and growing the art, and they, in turn, are learning and growing themselves. Don't get me wrong: if Professor Presas hadn't been taken from us, well, where would he be today? Wow! I cannot imagine how much more he would have refined his beloved Art. It was a painful transition to adapt to life and training without him, but there again is growth…

♦ ABSENT FRIENDS ♦

[With special thanks to Chad Dulin for going where angels fear to tread…]

During his travels, Professor Presas awarded several titles that fell outside the traditional belt ranking system. There is no exact hierarchy among these honors; ultimately, they represent a level of trust and endorsement of those he charged with promoting and preserving his art. Many students came into and out of his system over the years, and it would be inaccurate to characterize any one person or group as having the "true" art or way. It is far more productive, and more in line with the Professor's vision, to accept that there are many pieces of his art out in the world. The industrious student should have no difficulty connecting with any number of instructors and assembling these pieces to gain a deeper perspective on the art.

In compiling this work, invitations to contribute material were widely disseminated, and were specifically extended to at least one representative from every major branch of Modern Arnis known to the Editors. Everyone who chose to participate was welcome, subject to the proviso that no negative or self-promoting material would be accepted. And it is a testament to the Professor's legacy that the banners of so many disparate clans have come together within these pages—some for the first time—in order to honor him.

Inevitably, however, there are a few gaps in the ranks. Some senior practitioners have now passed on. Others have retired from the arts. Others may not have been aware of the open invitation to contribute to this project. And still others may have preferred not to add their voices to this chorus. But this does not mean that they should not be heard at all. It is the intent of this work to provide a broad insight into those who helped to shape and preserve the art of Modern Arnis, both within the Professor's lifetime and beyond. Accordingly, brief and respectful reference is made to certain distinguished colleagues whose own words, for whatever reason, could not be reproduced herein.

THE DATUS

Only six people were awarded the title "Datu" by Remy Presas. These individuals received the Professor's blessing to create their own organizations.

⊗ **Shishir Inocalla:** Currently based in the Philippines, his contribution is featured earlier in this work.

⊗ **Kelly Worden:** Currently based in the Seattle area, his contribution is featured earlier in this work.

⊗ **Ric "Bong" Jornales:** Datu Jornales is the founder and headmaster of the Philippines-based Jornales System, which teaches the use of the rattan cane and various other weapons, along with empty hand striking, kicking, grappling and forms. Datu Jornales has black belts in many different martial arts, and has won countless awards and titles over his many years of practice and competition. A member of the editorial staff who had the opportunity to train with him describes him as, "an intently focused martial athlete who impresses with his skill across different categories of weapons systems."

⊗ **Dieter Knuttel:** Currently based in Germany, his contribution is featured earlier in this work.

⊗ **Tim Hartman:** Currently based in New York, his contribution is featured earlier in this work.

⊗ **David Hoffman:** Datu Hoffman, the Professor's UK representative, was one of the first Modern Arnis black belts. The Editors believe that Datu Hoffman may no longer be actively teaching.

THE MASTERS OF TAPI-TAPI

Only seven people were awarded the title "Master of Tapi-Tapi" by Remy Presas. These individuals were appointed by the Professor to continue to lead the International Modern Arnis Federation (IMAF) after his passing.

ARNIS

IMAF, LLC

- **Ken Smith:** Master Smith, an Illinois-based Modern Arnis teacher with senior instructor certification in a variety of systems, together with Masters Chuck Gauss, Brian Zawilinski, and Gaby Roloff, comprise the board of directors of the International Modern Arnis Federation **(IMAF, LLC)**. Master Smith's many contributions are featured throughout this work.

- **Chuck Gauss:** A police officer for twenty-plus years and a student of many different martial arts, Master Gauss brings real-world know-how and practical self-defense techniques to his classes in Michigan and seminars around the world.

- **Brian Zawilinski:** A corrections officer for twenty-plus years with instructor rank in several disciplines, Master Zawilinski has blended his expertise to form "TAWA"—the art within your art—which he teaches at his school in Connecticut and on the seminar circuit. His his contribution is featured earlier in this work.

- **Gaby Roloff:** Master Roloff has trained exclusively in Modern Arnis since 1985 and teaches regularly in Hamburg, Germany, and elsewhere in Europe.

- **Dr. Randi Schea:** Prior to his passing, the Professor designated Master Schea as a "co-Grandmaster" (along with Master Delaney). Master Schea was originally affiliated with the IMAF, LLC, but his current whereabouts and teaching/training status are unknown.

- **Jim Ladis:** While Master Ladis no longer teaches regularly, he continues to improve the skills of his senior students in the Chicago area and shares his knowledge of Modern Arnis at seminars from time-to-time.

IMAF Inc.

- **Jeff Delaney:** Prior to his passing, the Professor designated Master Delaney as a "co-Grandmaster" (along with Master Shea). Following a split from the other Masters of Tapi-Tapi, Master Delaney became the head of the International Modern Arnis Foundation, Incorporated **(IMAF, Inc.)**, and continues to teach the art at a variety of venues both within the United States and abroad.

PHILIPPINES

As noted at the outset, out of respect for the Presas family, the Editors sought and received the blessing of the Professor's family—through Dr. Remy Presas Junior—before they began assembling this work. They have also connected with other Philippines-based practitioners of the art, such as Shishir Inocalla and Rick "Bong" Jornales, so as to pay appropriate respect to the masters of the country from which the art originally sprang.

Some other notable Filipino masters with a Modern Arnis heritage include:

⊗ **Jerry de la Cruz:** After initially studying karate for some time, Jerry de la Cruz began training with Professor Presas in the mid-Sixties, and went on to be one of the most senior Modern Arnis instructors in Philippines, teaching the art at schools and even on military bases. He eventually founded his own system—Arnis Cruzada—in 1995.

⊗ **Bambit Dulay:** Samuel Bambit Dulay started training in the FMA in the late Sixties under two students of Professor Presas. He went on to study with the Maestro himself, and showed great interest in mastering *Tapi-Tapi*. Eventually, he became the chief instructor for the International Modern Arnis Federation, Philippines (IMAF-P).

⊗ **Rene Tongson:** Rene Tongson began training with Roberto Presas at the age of fifteen. He went on to train with Ernesto Presas, under whose tutelage he refined his mastery of Filipino weaponry. He is one of the most senior members of the IMAF-P.

⊗ **Rodel Dagooc:** Rodel Dagooc began his Modern Arnis training under Remy Presas in 1969. Among his favorite techniques is *Ocho-Ocho*, which he believes to be both practical and effective. He went on to become known as "the Smoking Stick" and subsequently founded an FMA supply company of the same name in the Philippines.

⊗ **Roland Dantes:** A police officer, actor, and body-builder who trained with the Professor for over thirty years, Roland Dantes made great efforts to unite the Modern Arnis community during his lifetime and passed away in 2009.

⊗ **Vicente Sanchez**: Vicente "Vic" Sanchez met Professor Presas through Roland Dantes. The two became fast friends and frequent training partners. He went on to earn master rank in four different styles, but continues to teach Modern Arnis as part of his overall system. He is a member of the Modern Arnis Senior Masters Council.

⊗ **Cristino Vasquez:** A cousin of the Professor's, Cristino Vasquez began studying with the Presas family at the age of thirteen. Among his favorite techniques are the classical striking styles (*Abanico, Banda y Banda, Palis-Palis*, and so on). To these, he has added his own innovation—*Ipit-Pilipit* (finger locking). He is a member of both IMAF-P and the Council of Masters.

INDEPENDENT

In keeping with many of Professor Presas's directives, including: *"Find the art within your art,"* and *"Make it your own,"* many of his senior students have gone on to teach Modern Arnis independently, sometimes as a free-standing art-form, and other times, in combination with additional arts. Many of these independent instructors have already graciously contributed to this work. Others include:

⊗ **Jim and Judy Clapp:** Senior Arnis instructors, Jim and Judy Clapp were instrumental in arranging the early Modern Arnis seminars that helped the art to establish its roots in the United States.

FILIPINO WARRIORS

NOW YOU ARE HOME

Now you are home
Nepa leaves surround you

Now you have returned
To the shores of your mother
The mountains of your father
Infinity

Now you have become the weaving
Patterns of rattan
Playing among us

I hear you laugh
Let me see you do this, you said

You know it already
Unfolding the magic
Of hard work like silk
Scarves from your sleeve

I hear the tide
Whisper on sand

Oceans are the lungs
Of the earth you knew
These waves the way
To remember
We breathe returning

Always to the place
That made us—Tapi Tapi,
Palis Palis, Abanico, The Flow—

You could do this, you said
Or this, so many innovations

You shared a language
Of hands your ancestors
Spoke through you

Make the connections
In real, you said
That's what we're after

—Janet E. Aalfs. Dayang Anim

ARNIS

XX. THE FUTURE OF THE ART
Along This Way...

With the Professor's passing, the burning question is what will become of his art? During his lifetime, he awarded leadership positions to many of his students, including conventional ranks (degrees of black belt) and titles (including Datu and Master of Tapi-Tapi). He even encouraged some to go their own way, to found their own systems, with his teachings and his blessing. In addition, he was survived by various family members who practice the art, including his son, Remy Presas Junior, and his brother, Roberto Presas. The reality, however, is that Modern Arnis has not been unified under a single leader since 2001, and may never be again.

*****

The Professor always managed to find the beauty in what was around him. Once, while being driven from the airport to a seminar along a busy stretch of highway, he shouted, *"Stop the car!"* The driver, thinking some emergency was taking place, slammed on the brakes and wrenched the car off the road. Without batting an eye, the Professor jumped out and trotted back a few hundred feet along the shoulder. By the time the student caught up with him, the dust from their sudden halt was only just beginning to settle and the Professor was standing next to a guard-rail overlooking a lush, green field. In the middle of the meadow, like a centerpiece, stood a cherry tree in full blossom.

"The tree," the he remarked nonchalantly, *"it is beautiful..."*

And with that, he sauntered back to the car and took his place in the passenger seat as though nothing out of the ordinary had happened. And perhaps for him, it hadn't.

*****

In keeping with the Professor's extraordinary ability to see the best in the world around him, perhaps the fact that there are many fountainheads from which the art of Modern Arnis now flows is a fitting tribute to the way he taught. Like a modern day Johnny Appleseed, he traveled the country—and indeed the world—planting his art in many places along the way. And even if the orchards that grew from these seeds now differ from each other in significant ways, the Professor would still no doubt have been proud of the unique beauty and rich bounty that each has brought to the martial landscape since his departure.

ARNIS

XXI. THE WORDS OF THE MASTER
If You Can Imagine, You Can Make It Happen

There is an apocryphal story that attributes the origin of some of the distinctive consonant sounds in Castilian Spanish—such as the very word *'Cath-tilian'*—to generations of speakers attempting to emulate the idiosyncratic speech patterns of a historic ruler (possibly Peter of Castile). Whether or not this historical account is entirely accurate, it is inescapable that those who had the pleasure of training with Professor Presas tend to channel his voice and mannerisms when teaching. It is frequently unintentional, and always done with respect, but first generation instructors often find themselves saying, *"Could you do dat? I'd like to see you do dat! First, make it slooow… then, make it faster!"*

Other expressions the Professor commonly used will strike a chord in those who knew him well, and, in fact, provide a pretty comprehensive overview of the philosophical and practical principles that underpin the art:

⊗ Let the stick do the talking.
　⊗ There is only one way—that is my way!
　　⊗ It is all the same.
　　　⊗ Make the innovation.
　　　　⊗ You are part of my family now.
　　　　　⊗ In real…
　　　　　　⊗ Find the art within your art.
　　　　　　　⊗ Go with the flow!
　　　　　　　　⊗ We call it 'sharing'.
　　　　　　　　　⊗ Make it your own.
　　　　　　　　　　⊗ You have it already!

—Remy Amador Presas, 1936-2001

While the Professor has now spoken and written all the words he ever will in this life, the lessons he taught live on, and continue to show the way.

*****

At an Arnis seminar in 2016, a longtime student of the Professor's was demonstrating a disarm in which one of the practitioners holds his cane in a low, San Miguel-style guard position, and the other strikes down sharply on the stick, causing the *punta* to contact the ground and become a fulcrum with which to lever the weapon from the adversary's grasp.

At that exact moment, a connection was finally made for another first generation student in attendance who had learned this style of striking (a variation on "Planting the Rice") from the Professor himself years ago, but had never really understood its application.

And so it was that another piece of the puzzle snapped into place.

A once blurry image came into sharp focus.

A dormant seed blossomed.

Decades after its initial transmission, a message from the Professor was finally deciphered by one of his students. In this small way, fifteen years after his passing, his teachings remained very much alive. A root took hold. The universal flow continued. And in the end, wasn't that the very point of the gift he gave us?

—*Maraming Salamat*

ARNIS

YOUR MODERN ARNIS JOURNAL

◆   ◆

My Modern Arnis journey began... _____

ARNIS

ARNIS

APPENDIX A—THE FIRST TREATISE

Mga Karunungan sa Larong Anis by Placido Yambao (1957):

Nuong unang panahon ang mga Pilipino ay hindi nakikilala ang baril, kaya't ang sining ng larong arnis ang kanilang pinagsumikapang pagsanayan bilang pananggol sa sarili laban sa ano mang mga pagkakataon. Ang mga kaunaunahang nagging bihasa at sanay sa larong ito'y dili iba kundi ang mga rajah at mga maharlika sa kabisayaan at Katagalugan, Amandakwa sa Pangasinan, at Baruwang sa Kagayan, kaya't ang kali o arnis ay kinilala nuong unang dako ay laro ng mga hari. Ang mga bantog sa tapang nuong unang dako ay nakilala sa kanilang kahusayan sa paggamit ng mga tabak, kampilanm balaraw, sibat at pana...

"In ancient times, firearms were not known to the Filipino people, so the art that they used to defend themselves in all situations was Arnis. The most skillful practitioners of the art were the nobles, so Arnis became known as "the Game of Kings." Arnisadors became known for their superior skill with swords, knives, spears, and arrows…"

—<u>Mga Karunungan sa Larong</u>, page 11.

APPENDIX B—MODERN ESCRIMA

LEO FONG'S MODERN ESCRIMA
"MAKE IT YOUR OWN"

After meeting Remy Presas while shooting a movie in the Philippines in 1974, and training with him extensively there, Leo Fong returned to the United States, where he continued to study the Filipino Martial Arts, both by practicing and developing what the Professor had taught him, and also by becoming a student of Angel Cabales, the founder of Serrada Escrima.

GRANDMASTERS ANGEL CABALES AND LEO FONG

Over time, Leo developed his own style of stick-fighting system which he called: "Modern Escrima." This hybrid style retains many of the techniques and characteristics of Modern Arnis. In fact, Leo went so far as to integrate FMA footwork into his own empty-hand system—*Wei Kuen Do* (the Way of the Integrated Fist)—as well. Consistent with the Professor's injunction to "make it your own," however, there are some notable differences...

MODERN ESCRIMA

⊗ While Modern Escrima, like Modern Arnis, employs twelve basic strikes, they are not quite identical. The three that appear only in the Modern Escrima version (left wrist, right wrist, rising) can, however, be "tacked on" to the end of the Professor's basic twelve, almost like a finishing flourish, so that the student can practice both versions without doing unnecessary violence to either.

Reprinted from *Inside Kung Fu* with kind permission of Dave Cater.

From the on-guard position (1), Davis attacks with a double-hand overhead strike (2), which Fong deflects to the side. Fong drops down and connects with a strike to the knee (3). Fong continues with a strike to the back of the knee (4). Fong ends the technique with a strike to the shoulder (5).

ARNIS

⊗ Among the innovations of Modern Arnis is *avoiding* striking the hands, at least in training. Modern Escrima, by contrast, *emphasizes* striking the hand, the wrist, and the knuckles when appropriate.

From the on guard (1), Anthony Davis attacks with an overhead right. Leo Fong steps to the side and with the left hand directs Davis' force forward (2). Fong counterattacks Davis' wrist (3). Fong follows through with a strike to the elbow (4) and continues with a strike to the chin (5).

⊗ The "short striking" of Modern Escrima employs limited movements so as to avoid telegraphing, and a single, shorter cane.

⊗ Modern Escrimadors sometimes practice a thirteenth strike, derived from a technique perfected by Angel Cabales, who used to perform a unique, overhead cane attack with a rotation that made it appear that the stick *came out of nowhere...*

From the ready position (1), Davis attacks with an overhead strike (2). Fong cross-blocks, then traps Davis' hand. Fong counters with a rib strike (3). He continues the flow and strikes Davis' elbow. He moves Davis' arm to position him for a stick choke (4). Fong moves in for the choke (5) and ends with a stick against the neck (6).

⊗ Master Fong routinely uses the cane as a training tool. On some occasions its heft is employed as a hand-weight; on others, a padded cane is used as a fast-moving striking target. In addition, as in most weapon arts, many techniques with the cane have empty hand translations, and practice with the weapon teaches principles and patterns that can be applied to devastating effect when employed in unarmed combat.

⊗ On a deeper level, the relaxed flow and latitude for variation encouraged in the Filipino arts is the *sine qua non* of Wei Kuen Do.

ARNIS

MODERN ESCRIMA'S TWELVE (THIRTEEN) STRIKES:

1. Downward diagonal strike (right to left) to left collar bone;
2. Downward diagonal strike (left to right) to right collar bone;
3. Horizontal strike to the ribs (or wrist), left side;
4. Horizontal strike to the ribs (or wrist), right side;
5. Straight thrust to the solar plexus;
6. Outward rotating thrust to left shoulder;
7. Outward rotating thrust to right shoulder;
8. Upward diagonal strike (left to right) to right knee;
9. Upward diagonal strike (right to left) to left knee;
10. Upward sweep to the groin (backhand);
11. Strike to left temple;
12. Strike to right temple;
(13.) Rotating overhead strike to head.

Those who had the privilege of training with both Leo Fong and the late Remy Presas will immediately recognize certain similarities: Positive and enthusiastic attitudes toward teaching the martial arts; tolerance and appreciation of variety in the approaches taken by their students; and an overarching commitment to the proposition that training in the martial arts should make practitioners better, happier and more well-rounded people.

GLOSSARY

⊗ Ranks/Titles:

- Guro—Teacher
- Mag Aaral—Student
- Antas Isa—White Belt*
- Antas Dalawa—Orange Belt*
- Antas Tatlo—Yellow Belt*
- Antas Apat—Green Belt*
- Antas Lima—Blue Belt*
- Antas Anim—Purple Belt*
- Likah—Brown Belt*
- Likah Isa—Brown One*
- Likah Dalawa—Brown Two*
- Likah Tatlo—Brown Three*

- Datu—Chieftain
- Lakan/Dayang —Probationary Black Belt [♂] [♀]
- Lakan/Dayang Isa—First Degree Black Belt
- Lakan/Dayang Dalawa—Second Degree Black
- Lakan/Dayang Tatlo—Third Degree Black
- Lakan/Dayang Apat—Fourth Degree Black
- Lakan/Dayang Lima—Fifth Degree Black
- Lakan/Dayang Anim—Sixth Degree Black
- Lakan/Dayang Pito—Seventh Degree Black
- Lakan/Dayang Walo—Eighth Degree Black
- Lakan/Dayang Siyam—Ninth Degree Black
- Lakan/Dayang Sampu—Tenth Degree Black

* Colors may vary by school

⊗ Methods:

- Abanico—Fan Technique
- Crossada—Crossing
- Sero-Sero—Double Zero
- Ocho-Ocho—Figure Eights
- Redonda—Circular Striking
- Sinawali—Weaving
- Mano y Mano—Hand-to-Hand

- Banda y Banda—Back and Forth
- De Cadena—Chains of Techniques
- Halo-Halo—Free sparring
- Palis-Palis—Passing
- Rompida—Up and Down
- Tapi-Tapi—Counter for Counter

ARNIS

- ⊗ **Descriptors:**
  - Centro—Middle of cane
  - Debile—'Weak' of the blade (Spanish fencing term)
  - Fuerte—'Strong' of the blade (Spanish fencing term)
  - Kaliwa—Left
  - Largo—Long
  - Puluhan—Grip
  - Punyo—Butt of Cane
  - Corto—Short
  - Doble/Doblada—Double(d)
  - Hirada—Forward
  - Kanan—Right
  - Medio—Mid-range
  - Punta—Tip of cane
  - Serrada—Close

- ⊗ **Techniques and Skills:**
  - Bolo—Uppercut Punch
  - Dumog—Grappling
  - Entrada—Entering
  - Halo-Halo—Sparring
  - Hubud-Lubud—Tie and Untie
  - Kalas—Disarm
  - Pakal—Ice Pick Grip
  - Saltik—Snap Strike (Slingshot)
  - Sunkite—Arcing Thrust (Up)
  - Tulok—Push
  - Visidario—Transformative Flow
  - Buno—Throws/Takedowns
  - Enganyo—Feinting/Faking
  - Gunting—Scissors
  - Hawak—Holding
  - Iwas—Dodging
  - Langka—Footwork
  - Payong—Umbrella/wing block
  - Sikaran—Kicking
  - Trancada—Locking
  - Tusok—Jab/Poke
  - Witik—Wrist Snap Strike

- ⊗ **Weapons:**
  - Balisong—Butterfly Knife
  - Bolo—Long Knife/Machete
  - Dulo-Dulo—Palm Sticks
  - Karambit—Curved Knife
  - Baston—Cane
  - Daga—Knife
  - Espada—Sword
  - Talibong—Machete

⊗ Forms:

- Anyo Isa (Empty Hand)
- Anyo Dalawa (Empty Hand)
- Anyo Tatlo (Empty Hand)
- Anyo Apat (Empty Hand)
- Anyo Lima (Empty Hand)

- Anyo Isa Pamalo (With Cane)
- Anyo Dalawa Pamalo (With Cane)
- Anyo Tatlo Pamalo (With Cane)
- Anyo Apat Pamalo (With Cane)

⊗ Miscellaneous:

- Maligayang Pagdating—Welcome
- Maraming Salamat—Many Thanks
- Escrima/Kali—Filipino Arts Analogous to Arnis
- Opo and Hindi—Yes and No
- Ju Yoku Go O Seisu—Softness subdues hardness (Lao Tzu's <u>Three Strategies</u>)
- Pilantik—Overhead circling strike for close quarters engagements…

ABOUT THE AUTHORS

As with any list of acknowledgements, there is a fair chance that the Editors will inadvertently neglect to mention kind and valuable contributions from one source or another. In an effort to avoid any such omission, it should be recognized that this work is, in its entirety, the product of the collaborative efforts of many of Grandmaster Remy Presas's friends, family, students, and colleagues, and that each person whose name appears in this book has provided significant support to this special project. It is for this reason that authorship is collectively attributed to Remy's friends and students. Having said that, it is appropriate to provide specific recognition for several individuals without whose assistance this work could not have been completed at all.

⊗ **Chad Dulin:** Essential editor, constant companion, and itinerant instructor, uniquely situated to help 'unite the clans' in this forum.

⊗ **Will Higginbotham:** Seasoned captain with a steady hand on the tiller of many craft.

⊗ **John and Michelle Ralston:** Fellow travelers, both willing and able to lend a hand at every step.

⊗ **Ken Smith:** Patient mentor and generous technical editor in this, and many other endeavors.

⊗ **Dr. Charles Terry:** Steadfast guide and trusted companion on countless journeys.

⊗ **Brian Zawilinski:** Respected leader who truly understands the intent of this work.

⊗ **Friends, Family, and Followers of the Professor:** As noted at the outset, the true authors of this work are those who chose to come together in these pages to share their expertise, insights, and memories. In so doing, they recognize that all branches of this family tree sprang from a common root, and pay appropriate respect to the man who first planted the seed.

www.ingramcontent.com/pod-product-compliance
Lightning Source LLC
Chambersburg PA
CBHW051055160426
43193CB00010B/1197